TAI SOLARIN

Africa's Greatest Educationist and Humanist

BY DELE BABALOLA

Photo Credit: Newswatch Publication, Nigeria

Kwill Books Second Extended Edition 2018

ISBN 978-84-947548-6-9

Also available on Kindle.

www.kwillbooks.com

DEDICATION

TO THE INDOMITABLE SPIRIT OF
TAI SOLARIN

HONESTY, DILIGENCE, COURAGE
AND SELFLESSNESS.

TABLE OF CONTENTS

TAI'S CHRONOLOGY

1922 – ? Aug 20 (exact date uncertain) –Birth in Ikenne, Ogun State , Nigeria

1930-1941 – Primary education in various schools in Ijebu region of Nigeria and Ilesha; teacher training at Wesley School, Ibadan; pupil teacher in various schools in Ijebu land; typist appointment in Lagos.

1941 – Enrolled to serve in the Royal Air Force, WWII.

1945 – Demobilization from RAF in Canada.

1946 – Student at Manchester University, History and Geography.

1949 – Graduated B.A. Hons - History and Geography

1951 – Marriage to Sheila; Diploma in Education, London University.

1952 – Return to Nigeria; Principal, Molusi College, Ijebu- Igbo; birth of daughter, Corin.

1955 – Resigned appointment at Molusi College for 'Freedom of Religion' reasons.

1956 – Founded Mayflower School, Ikenne; birth of son, Tunde.

1958 – Fierce freelance journalism begins; regular newspaper articles for the *Daily Times* (1958-1967); and *Nigerian Tribune* (1967 – 1994).

1959 – Founded Mayflower Junior School. The first Headmaster was the late New Zealander, Lynn Richards.

1970 – In Eastern Nigeria at the end of the Nigerian-Biafra war to offer assistance to war-devastated Igbo people and to feed *kwashiorkor* children. He sponsored the education of several children from the war zone.

1

1971 – Commencement Speaker, Alma College, Michigan, USA. Honoured by the College with Doctor of Letters.

1974 – Detained for the prophetic bold article, *The Beginning of the End,* predicting the end of the military administration of General Yakubu Gowon.

1976 – Retirement from Mayflower as Principal; official handing over of School to the government. The school was valued at over 1 million naira but the government paid about a third of this.

1977 – Commissioner of Complaints for Lagos, Ogun, Ondo, Oyo and Bendel States; resigned appointment some months later due to "driving without licence" charge.

1978 – *Who's Afraid of Solarin?* - Drama in honour of Tai published and staged by the author Prof. Femi Osofisan

1979-83 – Freedom Square, Lagos; fierce open campaign against the inept Shagari government. Wrote the article , *'The Thieves who Govern Us .'* Wrote *A Message for Young Nigerians.* Joined Chief Obafemi Awolowo's Unity Party of Nigeria as one of the national leaders.

1981 – *Tai and Sheila,* a booklet on Tai and his wife, Sheila, published and launched by Mayflower, to honour the couple.

1984-85 – Long detention without trial by the Idiagbon/Buhari Junta; at various times in prison cells in Yola, Jos, and Maiduguri. While in prison in Jos, sponsored the university education in Law of one of the prison warders.

1985 – Released by the Babangida military government.

1989 – Chairman's People's Bank; resigned several months later as could not cope with several corrupt officials in high places in the bank. He had complained to the authorities and no redress had been forthcoming.

1993 – June 12 and afterwards – was in the streets, joining popular protests regarding the annulment of the June 12 elections in Nigeria, believed overwhelmingly won by Chief Moshood Abiola of the Social Democratic Party.

1994 – July 27 – Sudden death announced.

1995 – Tai Solarin University Ijagun, Ogun State named in Tai's honour – first specialized University of Education in Nigeria; the 27th state university and 76th approved national university.

2004 – Special 10th Memorial Anniversary hosted in Mayflower School to honour Tai Solarin – prominent at the event were members of the Humanist Conference – both local and international and eminent Nigerians and old students and staff of Mayflower. *Oga Tasere* , a book on Tai Solarin publicly launched.

2009 – 1st October – Abuja street in the nation's Federal Capital Territory of Abuja named for Tai by the government of Alhaji Umaru Musa Yar' Adua through the FCT Minister, Dr. Aliyu Modibbo Umar.

2012 – October 22 – death of Tai's wife and widow, Sheila Solarin (nee Tuer) announced. She was aged 88, survived by daughter Corin, son Tunde, several grandchildren, and thousands of her 'children' who had passed through Mayflower School.

ACKNOWLEDGEMENTS

I wish to acknowledge several people who had been very helpful and supportive in producing this work. The contact could have been physically or through their publications. I thank them all for rekindling in me the flame to produce this book. The first effort had the title of "Oga Tasere": frail, 'little master'. The new effort now bears the proper name of the biographee.

Specifically, I thank Richard Carrier (for his wonderful treatise on Tai on the internet); Mr. Leo Igwe of the Nigerian Humanist Movement who invited me to participate in the 2004 event in Mayflower, Ikenne, to honour Tai; Professor (Mrs.) Folabo Ajayi of the Kansas State University Dept of Women and African Studies, USA (a senior ex-student, an ex-May, ever supportive of anything having to do with Mayflower and the Solarins); Professor Wole Soyinka (who needs no further introduction) for his book, *The Open Sore of A Continent*, which he timely and justifiably dedicated to indefatigable Tai. His book had boosted my inspiration to write!

The second booster was from Professor Femi Osofisan's classic drama, *Who's Afraid of Solarin?* This world-acclaimed playwright had adapted the drama from Nikolai Gogol's *The Government Inspector* and the title inspired by Edward Albee's *Who's Afraid of Virginia Woolf*, giving the play a stamp of universality.

I must thank Emmanuel Kofi Mensah for his selfless services to the humanist movements and to the American humanist, Norm Allen, Jr., I express my profound appreciation for finding the time to visit Mayflower in 1991 and 2004, all the way from the USA. Professor Adrian Roscoe, in his book, *Mother is Gold,* expressed the fear that someone as great, selfless and dedicated as Tai might pale into historical oblivion because he felt Tai's essence would be buried in the browning pages of long-forgotten newspaper articles and therefore challenging people like me, on whom Tai had made an impact, not to let that happen by writing 'golden biographies'.

I must commend Akinbayo Adenubi for his timely *Timeless Tai* and Prince Sulaiman Bola-Babs for his wonderful volume of Tai's immortal essays in *Education For Greatness* and all ex-Mays for their collective goodwill.

FOREWORD

Dr. Dele Babalola did not meet me in Mayflower School. I belonged to the 1966-1970 set. I knew him at the University of Ife, Ile-Ife. When he came in as an undergraduate, I was already a lecturer.

We shared similar passion for Mayflower. I had spearheaded the inauguration of the Mayflower Old Students' Association at Unife when I was an undergraduate. Dele joined, and devoted himself to the affairs of the Association.

One other thing we shared together which I learned from this book is that we both lived in Kaduna House. The house motto was "Strive for the highest". This was a driving force for all students who lived in that dormitory.

This book thoroughly revived the nostalgia of Tai's Mayflower in me. In my opinion, Dele is qualified to write on Tai's Mayflower for two reasons. First, he belonged to one of the generations that witnessed the retiring days of Tai in Mayflower. And his account makes it clear to me that more than 90% of what all the earlier generations of students had experienced, which constituted the core tradition of Tai's Mayflower remained to the end.

I confirm this because my generation was right in the "middle," the 11th generation. (The school was founded in 1956. My generation was 1966-1971.)

Secondly, Dele belonged to a group of students we popularly called 'Omo Ogas'. This means *Master's Favorites*. Tai was the Master and we called him 'Oga'. This name, 'Omo Oga', was earned over time due to academic brilliance and high sense of responsibility. A number of events described in this book confirmed that Dele was one. Such students were very close to

Tai. So this book is Tai's Mayflower from the point of view of one 'Omo Oga'.

The details are very reliable and educative - even to those of us who were not that close to Tai.

There is another side of life in Tai's Mayflower, which Dele did not experience. In my opinion, it will be interesting to read about the experience of those who were academically brilliant, but are not 'Omo Ogas'! I hope someone in that category will have the courage to write because Tai devoted more of his time and energy to this category of students than the 'Omo Ogas'.

Finally, I call the Mayflower Dr Dele Babalola wrote on, which you are about to read, *Tai's Mayflower* because the present-day Mayflower School, Ikenne, is far from the original brand of Tai's Mayflower. **Oh, that Tai's Mayflower will exist again to build more men and women who could "HOLD THE TORCH ALOFT".**

ADEWALE SOLARIN, FMAN

Professor of Mathematics; COMSATS Distinguished Professor, UNESCO-Chair of Mathematics; Member, scientific Board of IBSP-UNESCO; President, African Mathematical Union. Director/CEO, National Mathematical Centre, Abuja.

WHY THIS BOOK?

Tai, even in death, remains a titanic icon in Nigeria. It is difficult to forget Tai. This book is essentially a sharing of personal musings and memories on Tai with the Nigerian public and humanity at large. I am historically conscious and I know the place of Tai in history (regarding his various exemplary, sacrificial and leadership roles as an educationist, social critic, national ombudsman, and freelance journalist with 'the caustic sanitizing pen') can be generously guaranteed from the chronicles of former pupils like myself. Professor Roscoe was certainly right in this regard. It is my desire to contribute this bit and make it as widely accessible as possible via the web, eBook, and traditional publishing. It is also an attempt by an old student, who was really very close to Tai, to share some intimate details of this relationship with a wider audience so that the value of Tai in our society can be much further appreciated.

This project had been haunting me for quite a while since I first did a similar one in my undergraduate years in the university: 1980/81 to be precise. That seminal work had been named *Tai and Sheila*. It was (and is) difficult to imagine and discuss Tai without thinking of (and including his inseparable life partner and wife) Sheila. Both had proved over the years be well joined together as the two sides of the same coin! With Tai's transition in 1994, when he weaved a dance, in the words of Wole Soyinka, to join the ancestors, this assignment had taken another urgent dimension - for one had to do an obituary of this champion as well.

Tai's beacon shines even brighter in death than in life –
now that Nigerians appreciate incorruptible, self-sacrificing
and highly disciplined leadership.

The initial title of the book (an earlier edition) says so
much about Tai: *Oga Tasere*. Both are Yoruba words. Tai
gave himself this appellation and he seemed to love
referring to himself as such. Dissecting these two words, I
believe, should help to unravel to a very great extent, the
kernel of the personality called Tai Solarin. For the benefit
of the non- Yoruba reader, *Oga* simply means 'the boss'.
Tasere means 'lanky, frail, simple, easily blown away'. Why
should Tai describe himself thus? This is a paradox. Tai
was satisfied being described as the lanky, frail, simple boss!
What humility.

Having studied him closely over the years, I could
appreciate what Tai was trying to say. He saw himself as
simple and plain as any human being could possibly be. In
that very ordinariness he had been able to make himself very
formidable in achieving the goals he had set for himself. He
did not acknowledge any outside extraterrestrial help for being
able to achieve his goals. He stopped believing in God, or
higher spiritual forces since the 1940s! In his ordinariness, he
seemed to be urging all humanity that if he could make a
success of his life then no one had any excuses for being a
failure! He had started out from the lowest valley of
commonness to the dizzying summit of the uncommon
celebrated national icon.

The Royal Air Force had been his posting during WWII.
He had survived the War and gained admission to
Manchester University by believing he could pass the test, by
listening to his inner self.

He had embarked on the Mayflower educational project because he had dared to believe he was pioneering and blazing a new trail in the educational field in Nigeria. He did not have the funds to start with but he was a very firm believer in 'where there is a will there is a way'. He forged ahead with his wife in pursuing the Mayflower vision, and despite very formidable opposition, he and Sheila did not 'break their necks' as a marginal note in the education ministry's file had prophesied.

In his frailty, Tai was outspoken, a vitriolic writer against oppressors of the downtrodden. In his weakness, he was courageous and unafraid; challenged various Nigerian governments whenever their anachronistic policies were seen to be harmful to Nigerians. Tai had fought against injustice, against man's inhumanity to man, against political graft, against bribery and corruption in high places. He had attacked religion; fought in the courts and did so much more. And he was *Oga Tasere!* Tai would philosophize: 'May your road be rough this year'; 'May you have a lot of adversity this year'; 'We measure life by loss not by gain; not by the wine drunk but by the wine poured forth.' If you did not like what he said, Tai would chuckle, "Why not just respond by telling me "same to you"!"

I therefore make bold to submit that through his actions, Tai was saying, " the quintessence of my life is simplicity and I value freedom and education. I may look so simple and frail as a broomstick. I am, nevertheless, a very formidable opposition to whatever or whoever I attack in defence of everything I hold dear as a human being."

This is the unscrambling of the "DNA model" of the Tai persona, the decoding of the genetic template of his essence.

We measure life by loss; not by gain; not by the wine drunk but by the wine poured forth.

DELE BABALOLA, PERTH
Western Australia, 21 July 2015

INTRODUCTION

OGA TASERE – THE CELEBRATION OF A COLOSSUS CALLED TAI SOLARIN

It was the middle of the night, and there I was, bellowing out old Mayflower songs, singing along, full -throated with the words thoughtfully reproduced in Dele Babalola's moving and evocative tribute to Tai Solarin, the visionary founder of Mayflower School, a revolutionary educational institution at Ikenne, Nigeria. Memories came flooding back, and although tinged with some guilt, I was transported many years back to those fun-packed, mischief-filled, rebellious, but powerfully influential formative years at Mayflower school. My house guests, whom I had woken up, came knocking on my door wondering if I was alright, must have concluded it was an end-of-semester ritual in Kansas.

Such is the power of Dr. Dele Babalola's captivating book, *Oga Tasere*. Numbered in 12 sections to include dedication, acknowledgment, foreword, and further readings, *Oga Tasere* has 8 short, substantive chapters. It is a slim book that appears to be an attempt to capture, and reproduce in print, the paradoxical essence of the man being honored in its contents. "Tasere" (smallish, frail) is the adjective the man himself added to the title of honor "Oga" (master, leader), that students at Mayflower School respectfully and deservedly bestowed on, and referred to him. As the author observes, such self-effacement is an indication of Oga's (Tai Solarin) humility. However, neither the content of the book, nor the man it celebrates, is lightweight in any way. Appearances can indeed be dangerously deceiving as many corrupt officials and unconscionable Nigerian rulers have found out to their chagrin.

The first substantive chapter begins with the end, 'The News' of Oga's passing in 1994. But it also sets the tone of the rest of the book – the significance of Oga in his students' lives especially of the author who can only be described as Oga's life-long disciple. Why is Oga so influential, popular, loved, revered, and cherished by his students? Babalola provides a myriad of answers throughout the book, but one answer provided in this chapter 4 prompts me to ask another question: What type of man, would say in the event of his death, "Wrap me up quickly and bury me. I want my body to be immediately available for decomposition that will enrich the soil and agriculture." This, especially in a culture where it is fashionable to keep corpses in ice for months, sometimes up to a whole year, and often for ostentatious reasons. It could be as an indication of the measure of the noted and the famous (corpse), enabling all the other equally noted and famed far and near clear their calendars so as to be present for photo ops at the burial. It could be to allow relatives and friends raise loans to give a lavish burial costing more than the deceased ever earned in a lifetime. Yet, Oga's order was "irrevocable;" Sheila, his beloved wife, companion, and soul mate buried him immediately, knowing full well that his beloved young disciples would desperately want to pay their last respects in person. Indeed, they did not equivocate, even though they still missed the interment after dropping everything to rush to Ikenne, the second they heard 'the news.'

In the next chapter, "At the beginning," the author introduces the reader, through the eyes of the author as a preteen, to general early impressions of Mayflower School and what it stands for. Like any preteen stepping into the sophisticated world of secondary education, young Dele knew all there was to know about secondary schools, and which were the best, not to mention the level of sophistication and elitist value. Definitely, Mayflower school was not one of them; it was not even on the list of the more prestigious schools he had taken the entrance examinations. Reading Oga's own account of his school, only confirmed his vague impressions this was a 'bush' school and definitely beneath his level. Thank God for parents' wisdom and firmness young Dele headed to Mayflower School, Ikenne and the rest, as he proves, is Oga Tasere, a tale of devotion, appreciation and eternal gratitude.

Another chapter that I want to mention quickly and very briefly is "Essential Tai." Generous, extremely principled, democratic, he engenders fierce independent thinking especially among his most fervent admirers. This is why Dele Babalola finds it natural and proper to criticize and depart from Oga's atheism and become a devout Christian, (86). Oga was a leader who lived what he preached; he led by example, not just a ruler. May dawn break on the day in Nigeria when any prospective public-office-seeking individual will be routinely conscientiously and publicly subjected to the test of leadership by Nigerian citizens. I totally and unhesitatingly recommend this chapter. However, as the Yoruba say, *"Won ni Amukun, eru e wo, o ni oke ni e nwo, isale ni eru ti wo wa."* (To the observation that the load carried atop the head was skewed, the cripple directed the observer's gaze away from the load, saying the top was not the source of the problem, rather it was located below at the legs). This chapter should be an inalienable part of every Nigerian child's library, from elementary to secondary; then, the prospective public official, especially those seeking to rule the country, can be meaningfully re-tested on this critical lesson learned early in life. What a glorious day that would be for Nigeria!

"Tai was a tough nut to crack," quips the author of Oga Tasere (14). With this work Babalola joins the many authors who have been trying to crack the Tai Solarin nut. I confess that I have not read many of the other tributes. I have no doubt that Babalola's book fills an important niche. The book delivers; we learn about, get to know, and appreciate the man of substance, Oga, and his enormous contributions to Nigeria at different levels, but most especially in the quality of education.

Oga Tasere speaks to anybody genuinely interested in promoting productive, and well- rounded education in Nigeria. Although it is a positive sign that the tradition of education at Mayflower continues after Oga's retirement, and after the government took over, the so-called 'Mayflower experiment,' should be replicated, and very boldly throughout the country. If it was an outlandish and foolhardy experiment in the 1950s and 60s, this is the 21st century and the 'experiment' has proven itself highly successful.

Read the list of highly successful, thriving products of Mayflower provided in *Oga Tasere*, and that's only from the class of 1973, the immediate experiences of the author, not the years before, not the years after. Just imagine how great Nigeria would be – nationally to its people and internationally as a respected world power if we had more Mayflowers! Of course, any idea needs to be regularly evaluated for improvements and relevance, but you need to read Babalola's *Oga Tasere*, among others like it, to know where the improvements will be relevant.

Take it from a proud product of Mayflower School.

PROFESSOR OMOFOLABO AJAYI-SOYINKA
Dept. of Theatre, University of Kansas;
Student Number 936, Kansas, USA, 2007

THE NEWS

I received a most unusual piece of news that day in June 1994. At the time, I was a private medical practitioner at Okene Clinic, Anifowoshe, Ikeja, Lagos - not far from the Ikeja Local Government Area, just parallel to the railway on its Iyana - Ipaja run.

My good friend, Wale Omole, a classmate and fellow old student of Mayflower, had delivered the news to me personally. Wale is the proprietor and medical director of T &S Medical and Dental Hospital, named for Tai and Sheila.

The news was very simple. It was short and it was traumatic. 'Oga is dead!' There could only be one *Oga*. I went into immediate denial of the event. My whole system viscerally rejected the very thought of Tai being the object of death. The name of Tai had become synonymous with life, not a name associated with mortality or transience. No, Tai couldn't be dead. This had to be a dream...

And talking of a dream, I had had an unusual dream only a few days before. I had never dreamt about Tai up to that time. In the dream, Tai was choking on his bronchial asthma and I was visiting him in his Ikenne home. His cough was rasping and agonizing. He was clutching at his neck as if without that, the effort of the tough expectorations might decapitate him. It looked that serious! And then he looked at me, very accusingly and said: 'Dele, my boy, do something.

Help me!' I was so touched for him. It pained my heart to see Tai suffer so much. The pain was so much that it woke me up. How pleased I was to learn that I had only been in dream land!

Now this: *'Oga* is dead!'

Wale was urgent, perplexed, sorrowful and resolute. 'I was informed only moments ago by telephone. We have to go to Ikenne now! My car is full and there is petrol scarcity. I know I cannot leave for Ikenne without you. Oga collapsed this morning as he was climbing upstairs to his study. He died in the hospital and if we don't hit the road now, we will surely miss his burial!'

Even in death, Tai was a tough nut to crack! Yes, *Oga* had always told us he admired the way the Muslims buried their dead. They wouldn't waste time. They would use simple raffia material and some draping and it was an urgent deposit into the yawning grave. *Oga,* loved this. 'Let no one give me any fanciful or expensive burial. Wrap me up quickly and bury me. I want my body to be immediately available for decomposition that will enrich the soil and agriculture! Don't delay' The order had been irrevocable. Then I realized Sheila would not delay. If, indeed, Tai was dead the burial team would be fast at work. How right we were!

I bade a quick goodbye to my family and nursing staff and dashed after Wale. The car's tyres were sagging under the weight of the several human occupants. However, I managed to squeeze in somehow. I could not take my car because I had no gas in it! Wale had managed to purchase about 100 litres of petrol at a throat-slicing price to make the journey feasible. His driver turned the ignition and in a little while we were zooming full throttle down the expressway to Sagamu! It all looked so unreal.

There were a few checkpoints on the way manned by mournful-looking, hungerstricken uniformed police men eager to delay us so as to get their palms greased with bribes. We were determined to honour Tai and ourselves by denying them. 'We are in a hurry to get to Ikenne. Tai Solarin is dead!' And that seemed to do the trick each time as we were waved off. Tai's name had not lost its spell!

Unfortunately, despite our rush, the burial event had been consummated. We understood that even the military governor of Ogun State, despite the haste he made, almost missed witnessing the funeral. Mathew Ogayemi, another friend, old classmate and general medical practitioner had been luckier. Mathew has his private practice in Ijebu-Ode and named it for Mayflower. He witnessed the early processes of the interment and even managed a few snapshots of Tai in open casket, dressed in green 'battle gear', complete with trademark cap and short pants. We had missed all that!

By the time we pulled up, we only witnessed the grief-stricken faces of workers, students and fans who had come from various locations to inter Tai. The grave had been covered and the surface adorned with beautiful floral rings. Even in death, Tai was a stickler for time and no respecter of persons. That was one unique burial in the annals of burial ceremonies worldwide.

Adieu, Tai, great soul!

A SYNOPSIS OF TAI'S LIFE
FROM BIRTH TO TRANSITION

Who is Tai Solarin? Why is he so important? What is the need to take time and write about him for posterity?

Tai was born a very ordinary human being. However, wending his way through life, he had seized every opportunity he could lay his hands to make his fortune and status in life better. He could just have lived his life as an ordinary Methodist-trained pupil teacher with only teacher training education level. No, this was not enough for Tai. He had envisioned himself going through the four walls of a university and putting that training to very practical and beneficial use of Nigeria. He was indeed truly a patriot. It is important to write about him because there are not so many who apply their education to improving the status quo of their countries.

Tai was quick to see the weaknesses in the Nigerian education system and the greater malaise of the political system driving the country. He swore he was going to live a sacrificial life to elevate the educational and entrepreneurial potentials of every Nigerian student that passed through the portals of his school, Mayflower. He was an inspirer. He was totally dedicated to human service. He mortgaged his fortunes to invest in the lives of hundreds of Nigerian students with great academic potentials but who were crippled with family financial poverty in furthering their education. And Tai helped Nigerians to see the malaise of the greater society and he had been very bold to write and cry out regarding what needed to be done and how to take charge. Tai cannot be forgotten for these services. He would also be remembered clearly for citing his life as an example that with a very clear focus, fortitude and diligence, nothing was impossible to achieve.

The exact birth date of Tai was unknown. A good guess is that he was born circa 1920. When mum was in labour and broke the waters, only the usual single baby was expected. The midwife was expecting the after coming placenta and then another bag of waters broke and the twin sister had followed! Being the first of a set of fraternal twins, automatically he acquired the congenital name of Taiwo or Taiye (literally the first to 'taste the earth'). The sister, in a similar manner was named Kehinde, 'the one who came after'.

His dad was a palm wine tapper and a kind of village minstrel good at singing and pounding the drum. He was also polygamous and had boasted that he did not know how many children he had. Although not that rich, the elder Solarin was blessed with industrious wives who literally slaved to look after their own children. Kehinde had cried so much, perhaps due to not receiving enough feeding, and this had irritated Pa Solarin to an intolerable level. He had to send Ma Solarin and the twins packing out of his home! In later years, he would suffer total blindness when while tapping palm wine, had encountered a cobra that spat venom into his eyes.

In 'exile', Ma Solarin was determined to get Tai educated no matter the cost. She was a petty trader and had very limited budget to educate her twins. She therefore decided to support Tai in the hope that when he started earning salaries he could educate and look after his sister.

In the years 1930-1941 he had to live with various relatives in different towns like Ogere, Ilesa, Iperu to complete his primary education and to proceed to teacher training at Wesley College Ibadan. In those days, admission to Wesley was fairly competitive and training was free on the condition that the trainee would plug back five years of teaching in a Methodist school to the community.

The time in Wesley College, Ibadan, was formative for Tai. Some of the traditions in this institution would be transplanted to Mayflower School, e.g. the school's numbering system for students and the seniority culture.

It was also here that he started to develop a sharp anti-corruption sensitivity to the Nigerian social life. The senior students were given money by the school in a roster fashion to do the weekly shopping for the school meals. They would shop and keep significant amount of money back for themselves. These meant meals without meat! Tai unmasked this racket when his turn arrived to shop for the school as a senior student. He did not short-change the system, but bought more than enough foodstuffs for the school and good chunks of meat as well! A number of his mates here would be friends for life – e.g. Badejo Ewuoso, Kalejaiye, Bolumole, and Bateye.

It is interesting that Tai started life as a very religious person that he even had to attend church in the hot afternoons. He had at least one reverend in the family who actually was posted as a Methodist chaplain to Burma (now Myanmar) during the Second World War. The genesis of his break from worshipping God and being a Christian began when his prayer to be posted to a big city like Lagos after completing his teacher training did not materialize. He had prayed so hard and the Christian God had not apparently heard him. How hurt he had felt! He had ended up in Iperu and later Sagamu, to complete the 5-year bond. During this period, he learnt to type as well. This had taken him only one week on the school's typewriter in his care.

This particular skill would later enable him to net a higher paying job at Her Majesty's Customs in Marina Lagos as a typist. This was 1941. An opportunity to enlist in the Royal Air Force and be rewarded with free university education if he survived the War (WWII) came his way. He was lucky to be one of four Nigerians selected. He seized this chance not because he loved to fight a war. There was no university in the whole of Nigeria in 1941 and the first one would not be built until seven years later in 1948 in Ibadan. Tai realized that if he could take a gamble and survive the war, then he could attain his dream of university education. And this gamble paid off. Tai would encourage anyone serious with his or her life to take this kind of gamble and leap without looking for it might just be that one opportunity in a lifetime to make it in life.

He sailed to England on the Tuareg. He was very lucky that the ship was not torpedoed by one of the numerous German U-boats infesting the Atlantic Ocean. The ship, however, was not so lucky on its voyage back home!

In England, Tai joined the RAF as a navigator of war planes and not as a pilot, as he failed the pilot test, not being able to land a plane. He did not witness active combat and managed to stay on the periphery of the shellings. He was demobilized in Canada in 1945, and found his way back to the UK to prepare for the English University education of his dreams. He passed the matriculation exam for Manchester University through a dint of serious hard work. He had dreaded mathematics initially, but managed to study hard and be disciplined enough to sail through in flying colours.

He settled for a history and geography combo. This was 1946. He was about twenty-six years of age.

Tai was very confident of a brilliant future ahead. He had great plans to serve Nigeria totally in the education industry. To learn more about the British way of life, he decided not to live on the campus but off campus in British homes as a lodger and he settled for one of the cheapest neighbourhoods near Manchester - Moss Side. This was a slum in those days.

He had several landladies and really savoured his experiences there. He had time to read several general interest and philosophical books by Bertrand Russell, H. G. Wells, Robert Ingersoll, Bernard Shaw, and Thomas Paine. If there was any residual affinity for Christianity in him at this time, those books and authors helped Tai to dispel them completely. He was now 100% atheist, and had fully sworn that his new religion was to serve humanity completely.

Tai would spend the weekends socializing, getting to know the English ladies, and dancing. He knew the kind of lady he wanted – beautiful, strong, very intelligent, a great reader, and an independent thinker. Sheila Mary Tuer fulfilled all this and more.

Sheila had been training as a chiropodist when they had first met, and Tai had been able to convince her that she would have to receive a University education to prove useful in Nigeria. How prophetic! Sheila turned out to be one of the greatest teachers the world had ever known and she would later be honoured in England through none other than the Queen as a Member of the British Empire, in 2007.

Tai graduated with a B.A. Honours in 1949, and followed up with a Diploma in Education from London University. He got married to Sheila in 1951, and, while Sheila was wrapping up her English degree in Manchester, Tai had to work in the morgue of a London Hospital, an experience that would prove very handy later when he returned to Nigeria.

Tai sailed alone to Nigeria. He had been invited by the illustrious educator, Mr. S.O. Awokoya, to take over the principalship of Molusi College, Ijebu- Igbo. Awokoya was headed for the Education Ministry in the Western Region of Nigeria.

Tai had to quickly settle into his new assignment, getting a very modest accommodation ready for Sheila who would soon join him.

It was not long before Tai upset the school's board of directors. The board did not like his mode of dress: shirt, short pants and sneakers with the big toe sticking out of a hole in one of them! He was encouraging the students not to go to church and to make thing worse, was allowing the students to pen 'dangerous' sermons in the new school rag. One particular article infuriated them about Jesus and Satan: Jesus arising from the grave claiming to have only been sedated and that he had not actually died!

By the beginning of 1956, Tai had had enough and called it quits with Molusi to found Mayflower School.

The story of the founding of Mayflower is the story of human will in action, of fortitude, of action and vision of a great belief in self and the power of self-actualization and positive thinking at its best.

Tai was about thirty-six years old at this time, and Sheila was thirty-two. They were both determined to face all odds, surmounting all obstacles to make the school project a reality. The construction of Mayflower proved to a great extent the tough stuff Tai was made of. He had proved this on potato farms in Switzerland where he had worked as a university student on vacation, harvesting potatoes at a faster rate than any other worker, earning the fitting title of 'human machine'. He was celebrated, and had his picture in print in the local newspaper.

For Mayflower, Tai had to sleep on piles of cement bags in the midst of a local jungle and slaved with bricklayers for days on end to construct the first buildings that became Mayflower School. The rest is now history.

While the Mayflower educational project might be considered Tai's main forte, his role as an unrelenting Nigerian social crusader was also very important. He had to physically remove decaying corpses from roads in the country and appealing to those in authority to pay better respect to the human body. He single-handedly fought for social justice like the instance when he sued a local doctor who was exploiting the townspeople, who would surgically open up the abdomen of someone, say for an appendectomy, and refuse to close them up unless his high fees were first settled!

Tai's crusades in decades of newspaper articles attacking various Nigerian governments for their myopia in not providing the necessary social services and infrastructures to galvanize Nigeria fully into the 21st century largely went unheeded. He would write and proffer solutions.

Tai loved H.G. Wells and he was in total agreement with the latter in the famous quotation: We are going to write about it all. We are going to write about business and finance and politics, and pretences and pretentiousness, and decorum and indecorum, until a thousand pretences and ten thousand impostors shrivel in the cold, clear draught of our elucidation. We are going to write about wasted opportunities and latent beauties, until a thousand new ways of life open to men and women. We are going to appeal to the young, and the hopeful, and the curious, against the established, the dignified and the defensive. Before we are done, we will have all life within this scope of the novel.

The foregoing is the best befitting epitaph I can think of for Tai.

THE MAYFLOWER SCHOOL, BUILT IN 1956 BY THE SOLARINS
PHOTO: KAIZENIFY

IN THE BEGINNING ...

I knew practically nothing about Tai until a few weeks before I gained admission to Mayflower School. This was in 1973, and I had just left primary school. I was hopeful to gain admission to 'prestigious schools' like Government College, Ibadan; Loyola College, Ibadan; Ibadan Boys' High School; International School and a few others in that ilk. I sat the entrance examinations for all these schools and then my father threw the bombshell. He said all those exams I had done were only dress rehearsals and that I just must get into Tai's school, Mayflower, Ikenne! A stream of quick questions coursed through my mind. Is Tai a Chinese? What is Mayflower? Where on earth is Ikenne?

I had not heard about any of these strange names before. But my father was adamant that the school for me was Mayflower. I took note of the name. The name sounded nice and had a botanical ring to it. In the innocence of youth, I wondered why it was not *Januaryflower, Novemberflower, or Decemberflower!* In my curiosity, I dashed off to Odusote Bookstore, not too far away, in Oke-Bola, Ibadan. I was lucky that day for I saw a copy of *Mayflower, the Story of a School* by Tai Solarin, conspicuously displayed on a shelf. It was not expensive and I quickly paid for it. That night, I pored over it; read it from cover to cover and digested it. What a book and what a story it had within its covers! Now I knew what the Mayflower idea was all about and I was now very anxious to meet Tai.

I was not too keen, however, to be a product of the school. Things sounded very 'bush' from what I had read in the book. The students seemed to do a lot of things by themselves. They constructed dormitories, washed their food bowls and had to do a lot of farming, getting hands dirty doing manual jobs. These were things I had been brainwashed were only meant for the plebeians in the society! Why should I go to such a school? My mind was in a whirl and my rebellious self turned really very bellicose within. I assured myself that I had to fight this out. No, I must not end up in Mayflower, such a 'local' school! I needed to go to a school where I would wear white shirt, white long pants, top-fashion coat, tie and blazers; where there would be no manual labour. I was hoping that I wouldn't end up in Mayflower. My father was adamant that the only thing that would stand between Mayflower and me was if I failed the entrance examination! And he was so sure I was going to pass into that school. He just knew it!

I traveled with my dad the day before the exam. We lodged at Sagamu Arms Inn and were warmly hosted by the proprietor, Chief Ogunmekan. I read the motto of his bar and was very impressed, 'Don't quit the bar when it is moving'. There seemed to be a message in that for me. Early the following morning, my father had to proceed to Lagos on business and he fully handed me over to the care of Chief Ogunmekan. The Chief was very avuncular, although much older than my father. He had such a nice warm and rich baritone which reassured and relaxed me considerably. He asked me to get into his Opel car and I discovered that I was *en route* to Mayflower with his own children who happened to be fraternal twins and were sitting for the same exams as myself.

For some reason, I didn't see Tai that day but took the exam in the large Schmid Hall and I found it was a piece of cake. I finished in no time and knew I had passed. I was too absorbed in the exam and knocked a little silly by post-exam hunger pangs that I hardly had enough strength left to explore the school. But I did notice the magnificent Administrative Block and the Netherlands laboratories. I was reliably informed that there were about one thousand students in the school and the teaching and non-teaching staff numbered close to a hundred. Communal feelings were very strong here and this was one spot in Nigeria where there was absolute detribalization.

My father picked me up later in the day and we bade farewell to Shagamu Arms Inn. Barely two weeks later, I received a letter in the mail. It was from Ikenne. I had passed and had been invited to report to the school for another exam - called the 'interview exam'. It was based on this that the final selection would take place. The exam went well and I passed. I jumped sky-high when I heard my name called by the late Pa Olusanya who stood on one of the tables in the multipurpose Schmid Hall to announce our names without the aid of a microphone. He sweated so much in the sweltering heat and I was somewhat embarrassed for him. This time, I was able to stroll around the school compound and studied the faces of some of the candidates that I knew would soon be my classmates. I had reluctantly convinced myself to accept the school, hoping that something good might come out of this eventually...

We were told to return to Schmid Hall for an address to the new students and parents by Dr. Tai Solarin. Yes, I was very anxious for the meeting! However, when I set my eyes on him, I was very disappointed at the Tai I saw. Somehow, my mind had been conditioned to expect the principal to be dressed in English suit, complete with tie and elegant sartorial taste. The Tai I saw was shod in a pair of white canvas shoes that had 'seen better days'. It looked like he was fresh from the farm or some physical exertion. He bounced into the hall, a good spring he had in his legs for a fifty-year-old! His eyes were slightly bulging and they swept across the length and breadth of the hall. Of course, his pants were short and of khaki stuff. His shirt was loose and swished freely around him. The buttons were partially undone two to the neck to allow for fresh air. He swung a long stick, marched in with zest and was straight as an electric pole.

In the blinking of an eye, he leaped onto a table and was now addressing us!

Oh, this is Tai!

He started to talk. His voice was rich and thundering, aided by the public address sytem. He congratulated us. He was full of adulations for us. He was very encouraging and blunt. He told us we were in for a very tough time in Mayflower but he promised us we would enjoy it. He reminded us that discipline was the watchword in Mayflower. Anyone who still needed to hang on to dad's or mum's apron strings was free there and then to return home and seek schools that would pamper him or her. In Mayflower, pupils got whacked generously when they misbehaved and there was plenty of manual labour: grass to cut, corn to shell, seeds to plant, houses to build – and the list went on.

WELCOME TO MAYFLOWER SCHOOL!

TAI AND BRITISH WIFE, SHEILA,
AT MAYFLOWER SCHOOL

EARLY IMPRESSIONS

I still remember very vividly the first few days of my orientation into the new environment that was Mayflower School. On the first day alone, we paid our school fees for the term - and this covered meals and lodging, school uniform, school books, school vest, the school hymnal - the *Merry Mayflower* - which I soon got very familiar with. We also collected our brand new mattresses and were allocated to our different dormitories. My dormitory was Kaduna House and I lived in this building for four years.

In my final year I resided in Oduola Hall, in the new dormitories for boys.

I found the school uniform interesting. The shirt was made of rather thick textile stuff with perforations on both sides to let in air. It was an offence to wear cardigans or sweaters in Mayflower unless one was ill and even then one must get the appropriate medical certificate. The green shorts were made of tough khaki material. The uniforms had been tailored ready for us. It somewhat reminded me of movies seen where new inmates to prison wards were handed their 'ready-made' prison garbs.

My first impression of hostels like Ibadan, Ikenne and Kaduna was to describe them as an abomination! The windows had no shutters! In Ikenne House, the window was just an open space and doubled also as doors when students were in a hurry to get out of the hostel. There was no ceiling. Aluminium roofing sheets were nailed on the wooden scaffolding and that was it. Whenever it rained, we usually realized we had holes in the roof and the floor would be wet. We would collect the rainwater by placing pails in the path of the raindrops. In the middle of the night, senior guys would wash their clothes in the downpour and drum on bowls or overturned receptacles to keep beat with the rain and one of the popular tunes was: 'Ojo *pewe koko, ko le ya ko ya!*' Translated this meant something like—the heavy downpour has drenched the cocoyam leaves, never mind if it rends the leaves asunder. We enjoyed it all. One really longed for those good old days. It was always an exciting feeling to think of how one had survived that period! It was tough at the beginning but one soon settled in to dig into it and to enjoy it.

One afternoon, during siesta, I was sleeping on the upper part of a double-decker bed. Junior students often slept on the upper deck; the seniors below. The latter enjoyed kicking, for fun, the boys sleeping above them! I felt a movement under my pillow. I woke up and behold I was face-to-face with an *agama* lizard. It even had the audacity to return my stare and nodded its head, as it was accustomed, to the bargain! I was petrified to the spot and the lizard eventually leaped off! I was too stupefied to make the slightest movement.

And there were the seniors! Seniority was a terminology in rampant use. To be one year ahead of another student was a big deal. You must respect the seniors or get punished because the rule in Mayflower was 'obey first before complaining' and it worked like the clock. The seniors enforced that everyone woke up on time, maintained general silence and helped to enforce other school regulations. There were many prefects in the school who also helped to maintain order. These were the Senior Prefects, Academic Prefects, General Secretary of all societal projects *(Dodo-Dindin,* Young Farmers' Club, Cultural Society, the Piggery Society, Citrus-Making Society, Cocoa- making Society, Goat-keeping Society and so on); Silence Officers; Chief Stewards in charge of food, *et cetera*. The school was organized like the termite colony and it was run very smoothly and efficiently. Students who were rebellious and who tried to derail the system were reported to members of the school teaching staff, who, in turn, would administer corporal punishment. Mayflower frowned strongly against indiscriminate urination - several whacks of the cane would correct this.

So many events to remember! I will try and give an overview of how a typical day went in the school.

On a school day, reveille was 5.30 a.m. The first bell rang at 5.20 a.m. and the second bell would sound at 5.30 a.m. sharp. Every student was roused from bed and expected to smoothen the creases on the bed sheets, tidy up the bed corner and be on the run for physical jerks, the early morning physical drill, usually conducted by Tai himself or some other member of the teaching staff or a dedicated senior student. Sometimes, students would not get up from bed during the rains when it was 'too sweet to cut the sleep'. No physical jerks occurred during those times and so students tended to abuse the waiver. However, Tai would be on the move; first to the girls' hostels which were nearer to his official residence and then to the boys'. All he needed to do was to whack one or two students in bed and that signal would ricochet like a bullet right round the four corners of the school, 'Oga is coming!' For this reason, many students never liked having their beds too close to the door! They might be the first victims to receive the unfailing whack of Tai's big stick.

School tale had it that some naughty boys planned to stop Tai in his early morning tracks. They therefore hatched a dirty plot. They balanced a full bucket of water on top of a half-closed door - an entrance they knew Tai loved to go through. Tai did not see the bucket. He was not fooled either. Before barging in, he prodded the door with his rod and down crashed the bucket! That was all the students needed. They knew it had to be Tai and in one minute the dormitory was deserted as everyone had leaped out through every available opening - window, doorway, whatever! They had escaped being flogged! Physical jerks usually lasted for about 10 mins. This comprised of hopping, jumping, singing, frog jumps, marching orders, imaginary rope skipping etc.

It was done in an organized manner for the various classes and roll calls were taken. The class prefect was ever armed with pieces of paper and pencil or pen to record the names and school numbers of students absent from the drill. This list would later be handed over to Tai at the morning assembly and those students would usually get caned. And finally, with a loud screech from Tai's whistle the students would be dismissed from the field.

Next was to bathe and get dressed. Mayflower had a bore hole to serve the school and this was usually functional and if not, one would have to take a quick run down the school hill, across the highway linking Odogbolu and Shagamu, down the valley through the rubber plantation on the opposite side of the road to the local Uren Stream. I learnt to swim in the stream for the first time in my life. I just got pushed in and had to gulp some water for 'starters' and to splash around amateurishly until I learnt the ropes.

One got dressed quickly for the assembly which was usually an open-air affair in front of the Netherland Laboratories, or in Schmid Hall if there was rain. The bells. The bells. Those bells! The bells were constantly chiming in Mayflower to drive the students on. There was always the warning bell and an interval of five or ten minutes before the final bell by which time one must clock the next engagement or face the consequences. If one was unlucky for the first bell to sound while one was doing a 'major' in the washroom, one had to control it somehow, tidy up and make a quick dash for the next event. In my time it was the pit latrine and the sanitary boys, under the able leadership of the Medical Officers, were in charge of maintaining the cleanliness and general hygiene of this place.

Students must be at the assembly ground by 6.10 a.m. Mayflower being a secular institution, there were no formal prayer sessions. However, in recognition of those with religious persuasion, Tai would grant a few minutes of silence for prayers to be rendered. This respected all religions and ensured no clashes or religious preferences. Thinking back now, I think this was a very mature and satisfactory manner of dealing with the issue.

We sang songs from *Merry Mayflower* and Tai might be leading the songs, or the Senior Prefect or the Social Prefect. Favourite songs were the school's version of the national anthem, *Hail Nigeria Glorious Land* and *Knowledge is Light*. (this latter song is written out in full elsewhere in this book). The rendition of the anthem was very good music to the ears. We were told this composition was submitted for consideration as the national anthem to the Nigerian Federal Government at Independence but was not chosen. The song was written by Hon. Denis Osadebay and music was supplied by the threesome of Phillip Gbehor, Dr. Sam Aluko and Tai himself.

Hail Nigeria, glorious land
Ever blest by God's command,
Land of heroes and our pride May true justice be thy guide
And thy sons and daughters be
Ever happy, ever free.

Great Nigeria we love thee
Land of wealth and liberty
We shall fight to save thy name
From oppression and from shame

May thy friends find all they seek
And thy sons be wise and meek.

May the Niger ever flow
And the green fields ever grow
In our fatherland and home
While the waves on beaches foam
As Nigeria s ensign flies
And our happy anthems rise.

We never sang the original version presented to Nigeria by Lady Lugard, *Nigeria We Hail Thee*. Other options to sing from at the morning assembly were: *We Can Become Whatever We Choose To Be* or visually-challenged WF. Henley's *Out of the Night That Covers Me* or some other songs. The list is endless. Following is the full text of Henley's song:

Out of the night that covers me
Black as the pit from pole to pole
I thank whatever God gods may be
For my unconquerable soul.

In the fell clutch of circumstance
I have not winced nor cried aloud
Under the bludgeonings of chance
My head is bloody but unbowed.
Beyond this place of wrath and tears
Looms but the horror of the shade
And yet the menace of the years
Finds, and shall find me unafraid.

It matters not how strait that gate

How charged with punishment the scroll
I am the master of my fate
I am the captain of my soul.

Someone now had to deliver a lecture, usually an
inspiring lecture or some piece of researched information
in the sciences, e.g. a lecture on the latest in space science or
a topic such as Noise and its effects as a pollutant in the
environment or bribery and corruption in Nigeria. Again the
list is long. Tai talked most times to encourage us to buckle
up and make something great with our lives and a lot of
these talks were 'richly buttered' with chapters from his own
exemplary life.

Members of the teaching staff also took turns to talk
sometime. Very often, senior students also talked on topics
they had taken time to prepare. They had to be very careful
of the speech delivery for everyone was out to pick out
grammatical errors which we referred to as 'throwing bombs'
and so one had to 'take cover' not to get 'blown to bits'!

A number of announcements were then made. Students
who defaulted by not attending the morning physical drill
would be called out for corporal punishment ditto those who
had made a noise since the wake-up bell, and other offenders.
Those scheduled for the Workers' Brigade for the day would
be announced. Students were also reminded to write articles
for the 'Class Winslow' magazines - usually about topical
events in the school, the country or the universe at large. Tai
usually gave every class a big log-type book for this exercise
and twenty of these pages were expected to be filled by each
class on a weekly basis and there were editorial board
members for each class to oversee this assignment.

By 6.30 a.m., the assembly would be dismissed and it would be the rush time for 'Ogi race'! This meant running, pushing, hustling to get into Schmid Hall ahead of as many students as one could so that one shot well ahead on the long queue for breakfast. Students usually had their spoons tucked into their pockets and it was not unusual during this competition to see a number of spoons fly out of flailing pockets as the feet did the fast jig to the dining hall.

It usually took about thirty to forty minutes to queue, pass through the serving area to collect the food that was hurriedly dished out, sit, eat, hurry through the inner recesses of the kitchen and wash up in hot liquid soap followed by a rinse in warm water before draining the bowls in the open. Next would be to return to the dormitories and prepare for classes.

Breakfast usually comprised of bread and beans; bread, cheese and cocoa; *ogi and akara or ogi and moinmoin.* All these items were produced in the school. The school had a bakery that processed raw flour into bread.

The first bell for classes would ring at 7.10 a.m. By 7.20 a.m., everyone was expected to be seated in the various classrooms. The principal had a favourite spot by which he used to hide in anticipation of catching and disciplining late comers. Tai was so good at springing surprises. He would lurk and blend with the foliage of a hibiscus plant, a perfect human camouflage reminiscent of chameleons. Late students would be chattering, trudging along or running. They would turn the bend and suddenly bump into Tai. He would transfix them by looking straight into their eyes to fully identify them. Tai probably knew every student by face. He would place a finger or two on his lip and hush the student or students to be silent and use his cane to point a place for them to join the pool of already 'caught' fellow students. Very soon Tai would have gathered a sizable number. They would get whacked and make a dash for their classes.

A student beat Tai to it one day. He knew Tai suffered from chronic myopia. He therefore refused to move closer to Tai when Tai ordered him to draw nearer. He kept withdrawing, very certain that Tai would not be able to identify his face because of his impaired focal length adjustment mechanism. When Tai then decided to close up the gap, this student made a dash for it, with Tai in hot pursuit, whistle blowing. The guy managed to escape!

Only students on Workers' Brigade were officially absent from classes for the day. They would be assigned to work with the school's paid labourers in the kitchen, on the school farm, at building sites, broom or basket-making, in the school bakery, etc.

There were several classroom blocks in Mayflower, an average of five streams per class. Since there were five classes — these naturally added to about twenty-five classrooms.

My class broke this five-stream rule because we were more populous at inception than any other class preceding us. We numbered about two hundred and fifty students and the average number per classroom was forty or thereabout. We therefore ushered in the era of the new Purple Classroom. The designations of the other classrooms before us were: Red, Green, Blue, Gold, and Silver. The most brilliant set of students belonged to Red and in descending order, the other streams contained the less brilliant students. Purple therefore was for the real dullards - at least for that term!

Within the first week of our settling into Mayflower, my class was treated to another set of examination. It was suddenly sprung upon us. Our performance in this exam graded our initial academic ability and hence made it possible to be allocated to streams. Secondly, the exam performance enhanced the student's place in the school numbering scheme. My number for instance was 2685 and it had stuck like a badge of honour to this day.

Right from when it was founded, Mayflower students had always been identified by numbers. Student #1 for instance was the first student admitted to Mayflower and today he is Dr. Oduola who holds a Ph.D degree in Economics. He had been honoured with a dormitory named after him in the boys' hostels. No dormitory or school building was named after Tai in Mayflower when alive, yet several school buildings were named after students, cities, overseas foundations and overseas fellows who had volunteered to help build Mayflower School. For instance, Owootomo House and Akinnibosun House were named after female academic pugilists who had distinguished themselves in the sciences (Medicine and Engineering). Among the males, Oronti House, Iruoje House and Oduola House were noteworthy. There were the Netherland Laboratories (a gift from the Dutch government), Schmid Hall (named for David Schmid, a Swiss volunteer who had rendered invaluable services); Alma Cottage (residence for overseas fellows from Alma College, Michigan, USA) and the list goes on. Humility, I believe, dictated Tai's rejecting the naming of any school building for him. He also declined the erection of any statue in his name.

Classes were held till 10 a.m. when the bell would finally sound for the commencement of the 30-minute break period and then resumed from 10.30 a.m. till 1.10 p.m., which was lunch time. Each lesson lasted for forty minutes. Tai encouraged the teaching of sciences He believed that this was where the future of any modern country depended. In Mayflower of my days and earlier, chemistry, agriculture and biology were compulsory science subjects. Physics was not compulsory but was encouraged.

All meals were eaten in Schmid Hall utilizing the same queue system. Lunch usually comprised of *gari* and beans; rice and beans (dubbed 'double decker'); beans and *dodo;* rice and *dodo; eba* and *egusi* or *eba* and okro soup or some other combinations.

By 2 p.m., the final bell for siesta had sounded and the school compound would be as silent as a graveyard as everyone took the compulsory nap.

By 3 p.m., the final bell for the afternoon prep would have rung and all students would be reading in Schmid Hall or doing homework. At 3.50 p.m., Tai or the Senior Prefect would declare the prep close and instruct on where everyone was to report for either 'society activities' or 'manual labour'. The societies had been mentioned earlier. Manual labour could involve being posted to teachers' premises to cut the lawn and trim the edges or to farms to weed the crops or to chop down firewood for the kitchen or some other allied job.

The activities in the societies were usually scored for the groups every term and these were recorded in the report sheets. Those in the Piggery Society, for example, were scored on how healthy they were able to maintain the hogs and their pens. As for those in the citrus fields, it was according to how much grass cutting, tree maintenance jobs and citrus harvesting they were able to do. In general, everyone was graded according to collective group performance in the various societies.

By 5 o'clock, every student was back in the dormitory and getting ready for the evening shower. Supper commenced at 5.30 p.m. Mayflower was very much concerned about noise pollution and it was a serious offence to make a noise at the wrong time. We were taught to speak in a whisper or low tones. However, between the hours of 4 p.m. to 5.30 p.m., one was free to holler. At 5.30 p.m., as the bell sounded for supper, everyone would be screaming and making as much noise as possible, to exercise the vocal cords, because after that it was golden silence again!

Supper would follow the same pattern for breakfast and lunch. The menu usually was like the lunch list. By 6.10 p.m., the final bell for the evening assembly would sound and all students would be gathered once again in front of the laboratories. Announcements were usually made by Tai, a member of the teaching staff or the prefects. Often, after this, Tai would enjoin us to sit on the grass and spend time in deep quiet thought, reading or to just remain plain silent. At other times, he tasked our brains to regurgitate some of the great speeches, sayings or passages he had asked us to commit to memory. Some of these were: H.G. Wells' *We Advanced Thinkers;* Andre Chamson's *My Enemy,* and

Abraham Lincoln's *Gettsyburg Address. My Enemy* was pretty long, but we got through it.

The school hymn book, *Merry Mayflower*, is full of songs composed by the students and it is updated every now and then. The songs are a true medley - hilarious, sorrowful, romantic, soulful, religious, philosophical etc. Years after leaving the school, we old students still relish singing these songs and they do bring back deep memories and feelings of nostalgia. Some of these songs will be quoted in some other part of this book for the benefit of readers who might not have the opportunity of browsing through a copy of the *Merry Mayflower*. For now, I am going to quote some of the great oratorical deliveries we learnt in Mayflower. Tai dubbed them *Mayflower Cathechism*. They must be learnt by heart and were included among the composed songs in *Merry Mayflower*.

The most popular, of course, was Abraham Lincoln's Gettysburg Address which read:

Four scores and seven years ago, our fathers brought forth on this continent a new nation, conceived in liberty and dedicated to the proposition that all men are created equal. Now we are engaged in a great civil war, testing whether that nation or any nation so conceived and so dedicated can long endure. We are met on a great battlefield of that war. We have come to dedicate a portion of that field as a final resting place for those who here gave their lives that this nation might live. It is altogether fitting and proper that we should do this.

But in a larger sense, we cannot dedicate, we cannot consecrate, we cannot hallow this ground. The brave men living and dead, who struggled here, have consecrated it, far above our poor power to add or detract. The world will little note nor long remember, what we say here, but it can never forget what they did here. It is for us the living rather to be dedicated here to the unfinished work which they who fought here have thus far so nobly advanced. It is rather for us to be here dedicated to the great task remaining before us, that from these honoured dead we take increased devotion to that cause for which they gave the last full measure of devotion, that we here highly resolve that these dead shall not have died in vain, that this nation under God, shall have a new birth of freedom, and that the government of the people, by the people, for the people shall not perish from the earth.

The world should be eternally grateful that the press had caught the gist and text of the late president's speech. Historians recorded that Lincoln was barely audible in his deep grief-stricken voice. What a great speech and what a great feeling for words, words that must have been strewn together from the deepest recess of his soul!

Then there was Elizabeth Browning's *Great Things Must Be Done Greatly:*

Great things must be done greatly
With a great purpose
A great mind
A great courage
A great energy and
A great persistent patience.

Tai always emphasized that last line on patience. He told us that genius was nothing more than 99% perspicacity and 1% intelligence. The inventor, Thomas Edison, failed several times at his numerous inventions. Each failure did not knock him out; knocked down a little, yes, but he was always bouncing back and learning from his mistakes and improving on errors until he got his experiments right. He was noted for many successful inventions including the incandescent lamp. This was Tai's favourite.

And there was H.G. Wells, quoted from his *Experiment in Autobiography*,

We advanced thinkers owe our present immunity such as it is, very largely to the fact that even those of our generation who were formally quite against us have, nevertheless, been moving, if less rapidly and explicitly, in the same direction as ourselves. In their hearts, they do not believe that we are essentially wrong, but they think we go too far, dangerously and presumptuously too far. Yet, what we live for, our sort, is to go too far for the pedestrian contingent.

Tai always stressed the *pedestrian contingent*. Tai had read everything from the pen of Wells: *The Time Machine, Tono Bongay, Outline of History, The Invisible Man,* several other titles and his final cryptic book, *Mind at the End of Its Tether.*

Tai admitted that this last book was very difficult to read. It was, it seemed to him, as if Wells was writing solely for himself. Tai remembered tackling the book in his matriculation examination into Manchester University in the forties.

And then there was *My Enemy* on which Tai really spent a lot of time urging us to memorise. He largely succeeded.

The drawback was that there was so much to commit to memory. The moral of the story was very clear. The passage was quoted from Andre Chamson's *My Enemy:*

"As I came down to the river, I saw there was a boy swimming about in the pool. He was naked, save for the handkerchief tied round his waist; as he swam with slow breast strokes, spluttering among the wavelets that receded from his path. Above his hidden face the close-cropped hair dripped with tiny drops…"

This story continued for about eight long paragraphs. It was the story of two sworn enemies: Andre Chamson and Maubert. Maubert was the one swimming naked in the pool and Andre was the one at a great advantage. Standing by the shore, stones gathered in his hands, ready to be hurled at his foe, helpless in the water. The latter had dared the former to lift himself out of the pool to dry land and risk a cracked skull in the process! Maubert had bullied Andre several times in the past with other street urchins, bashing Andre with a wheelbarrow on one occasion. This was Andre's opportunity to revenge and it smelled so sweet! Maubert was catching cold in the water and so was shivering with teeth clattering. He knew he was in great trouble and needed a miracle to survive. Andre got himself ready to fling his missile while Maubert panicked, imagining the very end of his life, but at the very last second, Andre had a change of heart, decided to be merciful and forgiving. He cried out to his erstwhile enemy to climb out of the pond, obvious to all that Andre was not going to draw blood!

What a piece to memorise! Some students got whacked for not being able to recite this whole story verbatim! It looked like Tai wanted us to understand the importance of forgiveness in life. He gave the story a very high rating.

He also encouraged us to read fiction and non-fiction written in English to improve our understanding of that language which is the *lingua franca* in Nigeria. He encouraged the reading of at least five to ten of books, in this genre, weekly. We had to summarise novels, drama or biographies read in exercise books which he could check on anytime. Once in a while, he would also take a class into the bush to spend time with them and analyse how they were doing with their extracurricular studies. Sometimes, he would ask a class to report at the Bush Library to write an impromptu essay which he would grade and publicly paste at the entrance to Schmid Hall for other students to peruse. These was usually a selection of the best marked essays, the worst possible and some in between. Tai was always full of adulation for students who wrote flawless essays. Mathematics was not left out. Near the teak tree plantation adjacent to the *Autobahn* German Road, was an old notice board with 'mathematics, more mathematics, much more mathematics' written boldly on it. Students were encouraged to write out their difficult maths problems here and as other students passed by, those who could solve the problems would slug it out! By 7 p.m., the final peals of the bell would go off for the evening prep and every student would be seated in Schmid Hall to study and prepare for the following day. Some of the tutors would go round to try and help students experiencing difficulty with their academic work.

On Wednesdays, prep finished at 8, and singing would commence. Tai loved to be there to conduct this session himself. Sometimes the senior prefects or some senior tutor would do this. These were no dull moments.

Every student usually looked forward to this interlude. The favourite song was *'Were lo ja... Eran sare wo gbo.'* This song depicted and rendered in highly colourful Yoruba lyrics an actual event that took place before we were admitted to Mayflower. The gist was that on a Mayflower Day (May 31st, to celebrate Mayflower and Madame Sheila Solarin's birthday) the cow purchased to be slaughtered to feed the school for the event broke loose from its mooring and fled into the bush. There was mass hysteria as everyone went in search of it. It was eventually found and had to be dragged, bashed and pushed etc. All these were recollected and amply captured in the picturesque song. Wednesdays were therefore very refreshing and worth looking forward to!

There were other memorable songs sung on Wednesdays. These were lifted straight from memory and *Merry Mayflower*. First was the school anthem composed by Tai himself right from the inception of the school:

Knowledge is light
And so the sages say
'For ever't will be the light
To guide humanity'
Knowledge is light
As ignorance is darkness
And therefore, Mayflowers,

Equip yourselves with armour of light
For our mission to the world
Is to bear the torch aloft
And cry with all our might
That knowledge is light
That knowledge is light
That knowledge is light

Just as ignorance is darkness
That knowledge is light.

Also inspiring was *I Shall Pass Through This World But Once,* which Tai had adapted from Stephen Grellet. The first stanza read:

I shall pass through this world but once
Any good thing I can do
Any kindness I can show
To any woman or man alive
Let me do it now
Let me not defer
Nor neglect it
For I shall never
For I shall never
For I shall never
Pass this way again.

And morally strengthening was Josiah Gilbert Holland's *God Give Us Men:*

God give us men- a time like this demands
Strong minds, great hearts, true faith and ready hands;
Men whom the lust of office does not kill
Men whom the spoils of office cannot buy
Men who possess opinions and a will (2ce)
Men who have honour; men who won't lie (3ce)
Men who can stand before a demagogue
And damn his treacherous flatteries without winking
Tall men, sun-crowned, who live above the fog
In public duty and private thinking.

Then, think of *Do You Know the Principal?* composed by Peju Oyefuga, a student in the fourth form in 1962.

Look around the school
And choose the right fellow
Look before you do
And don't make a mistake
He looks energetic
And works on with spirit.

If you want to know
Just sleep beyond the time
He'll come with his stick
And kick you out of bed
Sure you can't dodge it
Because of his experience.

'Come on boys'
Are his words to start working
'Alright boys'
Means that the end has come
He looks so brave
That you cannot just challenge.
'This student again! Carry him.
He won't die!' When he is very angry
He'll roar like a lion,
'I will beat your bottom hard!'
Students of Mayflower
Please cope with school rules
If it doesn't please you
He'll say you have to go
He is always harsh
With those who defy him.

And over the years, students have always enjoyed: *When we leave this 'merry' Mayflower:*

O, how happy we shall be!
No more ogi and akara
No more Wednesday's eve porridge
No more five-to-six get up quick
No more Saturday Inspection
When we leave this 'horrid 'Mayflower
It will be like leaving hell!

When we leave this 'wicked' Mayflower
O,how horrid we shall feel
No more stone, sand and water
No more ' Look here, your shirt off!'
No more baldness and miserable shoes
No more sleeping in class veranda
When we leave this 'callous' Mayflower
We should cry our eyes well out.

When we leave this 'monstrous' Mayflower
O, how happy we shall be!
Senior Prefect and Chief Steward
Cannot lay their hands on us
Barbers' Society, blunt scissors
Cannot reach our princely heads
When we leave this 'rocky' Mayflower
We should leap twenty feet high!

When we leave this 'lanky' Mayflower
O, how happy we shall be
No more chase from Migo-Meny

Mr. Bangwo cannot reach us
No more meat like mosquito leg
No more Olumo Rock eba
When we leave this farming Mayflower
We should holiday for a year!

How we had enjoyed those songs and those nights! There are so many more. The interested reader is referred to acquire the latest edition of *Merry Mayflower* through the offices of Mayflower School.

Prep finished at 8.50 p.m. and by 9 p.m., every student had retired to the different dormitories and by 9.30 p.m the final bell would ring for lights-out; then the drones of snores would begin to punctuate the air.

Saturdays and Sundays were different in a few significant details. On Saturdays, we rose thirty minutes later and moved on to the farms from there. We could put in two to three hours of strenuous farm work: weeding, grass cutting, log chopping, corn shelling or harvesting of crops. In some instances, we took a short break and had breakfast right there at work for the mobile kitchen would be sent along to feed us.

We returned to the hostel about 10 a.m. free to do whatever we had to do. No student could travel outside the school premises without official permission, requesting for the *exeat* paper. It was a very grievous crime to breach this school regulation. Other serious crimes in Mayflower involved sexual offences. These were not many. The weight of the punishment was heavier on the male offender, for it was instant dismissal from the school without any chance of pardon.

Between 10 a.m. and 1 p.m. we tidied up the hostels, washed dirty clothes and linen, took a nap and showered. By 1 p.m. we would be on the way to the dining-hall for lunch and by 3 p.m. we would be back in the dormitories again, this time for the marathon school-wide inspection conducted by Tai and the prefects. The essence of this exercise was to make sure all the hostels were in pristine condition. No speck of dust, cobweb, or litter would be tolerated. The beds were neatly made. The latrines and the bathrooms were also inspected to be sure that they were properly scrubbed and sanitized.

By 4 p.m., the inspection would be over and we were free to go for various gaming activities. Supper was served at the usual time. Saturday evenings were usually social evenings with no preps: film shows, travelling theatre, elocution contests, quiz, general entertainment. Sometimes, as it occurred once a year, election campaigns and vote counting were concluded on Saturdays. Yes, Mayflower School students elected their officers by the popular vote! Candidates for the various posts campaigned big like in the larger society and they tried to get grass-root support! Pamphlets stating campaign promises were freely distributed and posters and flyers with conspicuous photos of the contestants were also publicly displayed. The various contestants were also given the opportunity to mount the soapbox and use the microphone to defend their proposed programs and promises against their opponents.

Sunday was the day of rest. We were encouraged to rest and spend time in private meditation, sleeping, etc. Wake-up time was delayed for another hour or so. Next was the morning assembly, in the usual open air location. This assembly was different and the uniform worn by students was a departure from the norm. The boys had to wear crisp white shirts neatly tucked into green short pants, and well-laced white sneakers. There was usually the morning inspection. Tai would inspect the rows of students at the assembly, armed with his huge shears. He had a penchant for locating boys with bushy hair. He would approach the unsuspecting guy from behind and run the shears in two quick scissors movement. Large tufts of hair would break off the victim's scalp, hitting the ground, and Tai would move on with his characteristic spring to the next victim. This way, Tai tamed unruly boys to maintain their hair in a close cut.

The girls wore green chequered gowns with white lapels, smartly girded in the middle with nice leather belts. No fashion-statement braids were allowed. The girls either clipped their hair close like the boys or else they had to wear it nicely plaited or braided. Nothing gorgeous or dangling was permitted.

Boys or girls who had a different shade of uniform had Tai's shears working huge rents in them. Tai carefully collected the pieces and sent them to the kitchen to be used in the washing up of bowls! What economy! Some recycling! After the assembly followed breakfast.

Breakfast was served a little later than usual. By 8 a.m., every student was expected to have gathered in Schmid Hall for Community Gathering. This took place between 8 a.m. and 8.30 a.m. The Community Gathering was the school's response to formal religious education - for Mayflower stood for absolute religious freedom, in the true spirit of the seventeenth century folks who had fled religious persecution in England in 1620 aboard the *Mayflower* ship, across the vast Atlantic Ocean for the New World in America. The ship was akin to the ancestral spirit and guardian angel of Tai's school.

Although there was a chapel in Mayflower in the Methodist tradition of the late Pa (Rev.) Mellor, Tai had made it known to the general body of students that once they had the funding, he would make land available to Muslims, Animists, Hindus, you name it, to erect a place of worship. Only the Christians apparently benefited from this open offer. The relationship between Tai and Pa Mellor was very cordial, as strong as father and son relationship. Reverend Mellor had served the Remo/Shagamu axis with all his zeal and in fact, when he became very old and ill, he insisted in being transported back to Ikenne where he preferred to die. He had been reported to love Tai so much because in Tai he had seen the best practising Christian ever although Tai had long rejected God and Christianity!

Community Gathering was compulsory for every student. Those attending church service could only do that after they had attended the Gathering. Tai usually 'preached' at the Gathering. Other teachers also featured at other times. Rarely, speakers came from outside the school. The topic was totally secular in content. Madame Solarin had once delivered a lecture here on her belief in The Big Bang Theory, concerning how our universe had originated and Man evolved. The sessions were usually philosophical and gave the students a lot of food for thought.

Community Gathering would wrap up by 8.30 a.m and students were free to rest in the hostels, visit the chapel, return to Schmid Hall or the Bush Library to read. Noise-making was seriously frowned at. Supper was served at the usual time and prep usually followed. Afterwards, students retired to bed and got themselves prepared for the following day.

TAI AS COMMENCEMENT SPEAKER AT ALMA COLLEGE,
MICHIGAN, USA, 1971

GETTING TO KNOW TAI

It was every student's dream to be personally acquainted with
Tai. At what point in time Tai noticed me and stored my
image in his memory I would not know. In a class of two
hundred and fifty students, distinguishing oneself would not
be that easy. However, I do recollect that I used to regularly
receive his verbal commendations for being a well-read
student. It was not unusual to record in my exercise
books about fifteen to twenty slim fiction and non-
fiction books to be read in the course of one week. Tai
was naturally very proud of this achievement, and he did

encourage me and pour encomiums on me: 'That's my boy! Very good, my boy. You are going to be great.' That was pure Tai!

On another occasion, my class of students was brought to Tai to be disciplined for noise-making. Tai refused to punish everyone. He said there were some of us whom he knew would never be guilty of such an offence. He gathered us into a depression and he climbed a flight of stairs to the first floor of the Netherland Laboratories, and from that vantage position, he looked down on us and did something startling. He pointed to a few students and asked them to stand aside from the rest. I was among the handful so picked. I was initially scared thinking we were destined for more severe corporal punishment! Tai declared my sub-group free and that the larger remnant would have to go with him to do some grass cutting. My sub-group was asked to return to the classroom for some private reading since we had free periods. And I wondered at the criteria that Tai had used to know who should stay behind and who should go for manual labour!

Tai nurtured my class of students, the 1973 set, for only three years out of our five years in the school. He retired and resigned from Mayflower secondary school in 1976. We were in the third form then. However, earlier in 1975, he announced that he had in his possession a few copies of the banned *The Man Died,* the prison notes of Wole Soyinka. He offered to lend the copies out to students who might wish to read Wole.

I had read a few of Wole's books and I appreciated him a lot, not only as a writer of genius, but also as an intellectual, playwright, political activist and satirist of the highest calibre.

He came across as someone sharing the same kindred spirit with Tai. I had read his *The Lion and the Jewel, The Trials of Brother Jero, The Strong Breed,* a few of his poems especially the hilarious *Telephone Conversation* and his novel, *The Interpreters.* Some of my colleagues complained that reading Wole was very hard going and usually had to abandon reading his books. I never felt that way. I really enjoyed reading him, although I must admit I had to use the lexicon pretty often because his vocabulary range was very wide and deep indeed. I was therefore very enthused to know that Tai had copies of *The Man Died.*

When I went to Tai, asking for the book, he frowned a little and stared at me; surprised. 'What class are you in?' His eyes popped to large saucers when I told him: 'Class two, sir!' 'Well, good luck then. I hope you enjoy it!' And he handed me the hardcover. I wrestled with the book over the next three days. I find it very conversational, intensely poetic, very readable and confidently informative. The author was such a wonderful word weaver! That book generated a very close bond between Tai and me. When I finally returned the book, he said, 'You know, a number of people much older than you have read that book and complained that they found it very difficult to understand in places. I am very proud of you, my boy!' And he held my hand in a warm handshake and gave me a friendly squeeze. After that encounter, I knew Tai would spot my face in a crowd.

As 1976 approached, Tai started building his retirement home not far from Mayflower Junior School and I was one of the students who volunteered to work with the labourers who built the house. Tai noticed this and showed his appreciation by rewarding volunteers like me with visits to Itanna Rest House in the secondary school, for rich sumptuous meals at his expense. Whenever we refused his generous offer, Tai wouldn't take no for an answer. This further cemented the budding relationship.

NEWLY-GRADUATED EX-MAY, DR. MATHEW OGAYEMI
POSES WITH THE SOLARINS, MAYFLOWER SCHOOL,
IKENNE, NIGERIA, CIRCA 1985.

THE ESSENTIAL TAI

I must say I got to know Tai more intimately after I graduated
from secondary school and spent some time, with colleagues
like Dr. Matthew Ogayemi, Kayode Kamson, Dr. Wale
Omole, Dr. Morufu Okunuga and Akintunde Olunu (one
of the best mathematical minds in the world) doing volunteer
teaching in Mayflower School. Tai was very proud of us
and was very supportive of the idea of our coming back to the
school to help the younger students in their weak subjects.
This was not a practice that originated with us. Some older
students of Mayflower like Professor Ejovo Ohwovoriole,
Dr. Kunle Ogunde, Dr. Kunle Eweje (legendary artist and
medic), John Mbonu, Bayo Ajewole (physicist) and Disu

Aponbiede (metallurgical engineer) had always returned to help out current students as volunteers. It was a tradition that Tai encouraged. He would ensure that they enjoyed their stay. Accommodation and feeding would be free. And there were always other perks, like good 'pocket money'!

Tai was ascetic in a way, and charismatic in another. He loved people, and also loved his solitude. He often told me that his mind was a kingdom to him. He lived a very balanced and full life. I studied him at very close quarters when he retired into his new home located not far from the Mayflower Junior School which he ran privately with his wife. Tai, by Nigerian standards, was bohemian in character, dressing mode and lifestyle. He was a well-read man and very urbane. He had studied the minds and actions of great men by reading their autobiographies in preference to biographies.

His heroes were people like Thomas Paine, Robert Ingersoll, Bertrand Russell, H.G. Wells, Hugh Gaitskell, Jawaharlal Nehru, Mahatma Ghandi, Martin Luther King Jnr., Obafemi Awolowo, to name a few. In a personal interview, he once confessed to me that he preferred reading great men writing the story of their lives themselves. One would appreciate their personal writing styles, personal motivation for living, their religion, their credo, which the most astute biographer could never match or fully unravel. Tai lived simply. He made sure all the basic amenities of life worked in his school, although that, unfortunately, was often not the case in the larger society called Nigeria. There was running water and electricity. A borehole served the Students' Second Home and the Junior School; an older one served the Mayflower secondary school. This was well maintained and regularly serviced. The majority of students and staff lived within the school premises and the symbiotic existence was excellent. The tutors taught the students. The students' industry augmented the paid labour force. They cooked, constructed dwelling places, farmed. They handled the plumbing, electrical and other domestic and communal necessities. These would be great savings for any school. Tai never believed in getting a child so educated that the hands would atrophy from disuse. Tai's concept was that students should have sharp minds, believe in the dignity of labour and be able to integrate usefully into society and not be alienated breeds, living as parasites off other people's sweat.

When Tai was planning his exit from Mayflower School, he had already thought ahead about what he planned to do in his retiring years. He did not want to share the same access road with Mayflower. He therefore carved out a new road in the jungle to link his new residence with the main highway. He organized labourers and students to clear this dense jungle.

Trees were chopped down and before he was ready to use it as a road, Tai made sure corn was planted and harvested! He eventually named the road after his Nigerian military hero, the charismatic late Major Chukwuma Kaduna Nzeogwu who had saved his life from the bullets of his enemy in January 1966, by staging the first Nigerian *coup d'etat.*

To cater for parents who lived far from Ikenne and who desired that their children have access to Mayflower unique education, Tai constructed the Students' Second Home which now served Mayflower School boarding tradition to resident students. When Government fully took over Mayflower and paid out the 350,000 naira compensation, the school had become a day school with boarding facility scrapped. Tai's response to this dire need therefore was the Students' Second Home. This new institution actually served, apart from Mayflower students, other students in two nearby schools - Ikenne Community High School and United High School.

With the compensation money in tow, Tai gave cash gifts to labourers who had served Mayflower from her inception. He invested the rest in a large rental apartment building in Owonrosoki, Lagos. This new investment was named Mayflower House. A large portion of the returns on this investment was still donated to assist indigent students in Mayflower School and also to subsidize the financial needs of the school itself. Tai was a true visionary. He always had every step taken thought of and taken care of a long time ahead. He was indeed the quintessential advanced thinker and planner.

Students' Second Home is likened to a Mayflower School Phase 2 project. It, therefore, looked as if, although Tai had officially retired, he was not tired! The full tradition of the old Mayflower system is put to full use here in the Second Home. Manual labour and serious academics are still pursued as vigorously as before. Tai still played a very active role until his death and had employed able assistants to help instil the usual discipline. These assistants were Mr. H.O. Oduneye, Alhaji Adewale Bakare and Pa Aiyedun. They served the Second Home tirelessly.

Mayflower Junior School is still privately run, and together with Students' Second Home, constituted the educational business investments of the Solarins.

Tai was probably the only Nigerian of celebrity status who ran an 'open house'. His doors were open to anyone who wanted to see him. There were no red tapes of bureaucracy or security details. He was always the ideal genial host. If you met him dining, he would invite you to eat with him and he would listen to what you had to tell him. He would chat with you and when you were done with your visit and taking your exit, he would take you by the farm and harvest a few crops for you as a gift. If you were lucky he might further give you a live fowl from his large poultry to take away. He was such a generous spirit. He was one Nigerian of whom one could say, 'In him was no guile.'

In his 'retirement', Tai still woke up very early in the morning at 4.45 a.m. He still suffered from his bronchial asthma attacks. He would be at the Students' Second Home to drill them in the morning and supervise during manual labour. He made sure the students enjoyed their paid dwelling and the food service was superb. The school dispensary was well-equipped and covered by a 24-hour professional nursing service.

In the evenings, or whenever he had the time to spare, Tai would be in his study to write his weekly pungent *Tribune* articles. He would also find the time to read through his numerous fan mails from home and abroad, trying hard to write a reply to everyone. He would also read his books, news items and dailies as well as other literature to keep abreast of events all over the world. Tai's day was always spent as if there was no tomorrow. He was driven by the saying, *Yesterday is gone forever; today is action; tomorrow may never come.* He certainly believed that 'procrastination is the enemy of progress'.

On my numerous visits to his home, I always adored him as a great humanist and a very rare species at that. Tai would never ask you to do what he would hate to do himself. If he asked you to be disciplined, incorruptible, or honest, that was because he did not practise the opposite himself. He was very exacting on himself and never spared an ounce of energy in pursuit of whatever he believed in.

He detested waste in any form. At one time, one of the female sponsored students living in his residence burnt some slices of bread in the toaster and binned them. When Tai discovered this, he retrieved them and ate them himself in the presence of the girl! The latter was so touched and broke down weeping, heart broken. There had been occasions in Tai's life when he had had to eat beans with maggots or teeming weevils! Such things had never bothered him.

When he was founding Mayflower with Sheila, in 1956, they did not have the 4,000 pounds (not even 4,000 shillings Tai would say) bank deposit requirement as instructed by the Ministry of Education of the Western Region of Nigeria. But they had plenty of pluck and courage. And the Minister of Education, the late Prof. Awokoya, had written in the margins of the Solarins' application for the attention of Mr. Childe, the permanent secretary in the Ministry, ' Let them break their necks. They are still young!' The rest is history! Tai would always harp that if you had a laudable goal, then 'let nothing debar you'; 'keep focused'; 'whack yourself up'; 'pull yourself up by the shoestrings'; 'wallop the horse'; 'be persistent and dogged and victory would come'. 'No paean without pain!' 'Nothing ventured, nothing gained.' 'We can become whatever we choose to be.' 'You cannot make omelette without breaking eggs!' And when Tai was leaving

Mayflower officially in 1976, he taught us one new song, later included in Merry Mayflower - The Indispensable Man:

> Sometimes when you are feeling important
> Sometimes when your ego's in bloom
> Sometimes when you take it for granted
> You 're the best qualified man in the room
> Sometimes when you feel that your going
> Would leave an unfillable hole
> Just follow this simple instruction
> And see how it humbles your soul.
>
> Take a bucket and fill it with water
> Put your hands in it up to your wrist
> Pull them out and the hole that remains
> Is the measure how you'll be missed
> You may splash all you please when you enter
> You may stir up the water galore
> But stop and you'll find in a minute
> That it looks just the same as before.
>
> The moral of this is quite simple
> Do just the best that you can
> Be proud of yourself but remember
> There is 'NO INDISPENSABLE MAN'.

Tai taught us this song to let us know that he had played his role in the brinkmanship of Mayflower and there would always be someone out there to continue from where he had let off and even improved on things. How prophetic.

Mayflower's academic standards today definitely surpassed anything that was achieved in Tai's years. Mr. T.F. Odubanjo succeeded Tai and improved on Tai's work. Mr. Kujore received the baton and took Mayflower to another height still. He was particularly noted for his work on improving the school poultry. When Mr Segun Osiboye took over, he did more fine-tuning and sprucing. Mr. Osiboye was a Tai-enthusiast long before becoming the Principal. He seemed to have a clipping of every article that had emanated from Tai's pen!

Mrs. Modupe Morafa succeeded Mr. Osiboye. She is a lady of many 'firsts' – first female principal; first Ex-May principal; first American university graduate principal (graduated from Howard University, DC, USA). She is called the 'Iron Lady' like the British Margaret Thatcher and she is making positive waves. Recently she was honoured as the best sitting principal in the whole of Ogun State. This is progress. I wish our African 'sit-tight' politicians and office-holders will borrow a leaf from this example of leadership succession in Mayflower.

The overriding impression of Tai's lifestyle was his total self-denial of others; that other people must be served first and himself last; and that leadership meant suffering. Tai was prepared, like Jesus in the Bible, to wipe the feet of his disciples. His service to Man was total. He said he served no other God but humanity and that his gods and goddesses were the Nigerian boys and girls who altogether constituted the future of Nigeria.

One yardstick with which, I believe, Tai's greatness and relevance would be measured related to the amount of personal losses he had incurred in advancing the course of education in this country. He could have easily become a millionaire several times over but he chose to live like a plebeian to conserve the funds to educate the indigent but highly cerebral children.

If he met any brilliant Nigerian child who was financially handicapped and therefore having problems furthering his or her education, Tai would take over the responsibility of footing the education bills. There must be several hundreds of other people's children that Tai had assisted this way. He could not imagine himself living an opulent lifestyle while Nigerian children were being denied educational opportunities.

If he had only 'played ball' Tai could have held any portfolio or ministry of his liking in any Nigerian government. But he was such a gadfly, ever stinging the government in their most vulnerable areas, especially regarding the utter neglect of giving sound education free at all levels in Nigeria. Tai had agreed with Herbert George Wells that you could educate the whole world to the not-so-exalted level of a Cambridge undergraduate in a lifetime. But there had to be a will.

He never hid his disgust for the so-called Unity Schools which he felt were an unnecessary drain of Nigeria's scarce resources. Of course, education was not assessed based on the beauty and designs of the campus buildings but on the moral, physical and intellectual stuff the products of the institution had imbibed while in training. If elegance of school architecture was the only parameter to use to judge Mayflower School then it could not be reckoned with as an educational force and yet, Mayflower, today, is a great educational success story, churning out medical doctors, engineers, scientists, agriculturists and others in their hundreds in every cycle. And we must not forget that the first laboratory the school used was nothing but a cupboard! Indeed, Mayflower has come a long way. Tai was so unique and his Spartan qualities were unparalleled in the annals of Nigeria.

I choose to close this chapter by citing some incidences describing how Tai often responded to the needs of a fellow Nigerian, illustrating from my own personal experience.

It was sometime during my university days that I was the leader of a student organization. We were trying to organize a very important symposium on campus that required some external funding. The laudable programme was almost grounded due to the inability of our sponsors to be generous enough with their financial support. Tai identified with the program, and I passed by Ikenne, as I was wont to do, on my way from Lagos. I vented my frustration to Tai, as a friend, and he gave me a listening ear. He fed me, accommodated me in a warm room, patted me on the back and just smiled. I retired to bed and in the middle of the night, I heard a soft knock. I was bewildered to see Tai at the door. My eyes popped out of their sockets in disbelief!

What was Tai doing here? He only looked at me and smiled. What a smile! It was so genuine and was coming from deep down what people call milk of human kindness. He handed me a bulky envelope and before I could say 'Oga!' he had disappeared into the privacy of his bedroom!

With trembling hands, I prised the envelope open. Lo and behold, it contained five hundred naira! This was a lot of money in 1981, probably more than five hundred US dollars at that time. This was a real windfall and was more than enough to cover our expenses for the programme planned. I had not told Tai how much I needed. How did he know how much we would need? And why must he tax himself to give this free to us from his over-stretched purse? I was so touched and told him this first thing the following morning as soon as I ran into him. Tai only smiled again and patted me at the back and wished my group well in our campus endeavours. He was indeed a very kind and loving man.

The second occasion involved a very close relative of mine who stumbled on a rare business opportunity in Japan but could not raise the funds to pursue his dream and realize it.

Again, Tai came to the rescue; loaned him 2,500 naira in 1983 (more than 7,500 US dollars today!) to cover airfare and incidentals.

When the Dreamer returned from Tokyo, Tai, in my personal recognition, loaned a further 8,000 naira to him to enable the physical establishment of the business he had gone to Japan to train for. The sad news was that the proposed business never took off and this relative never bothered to repay his financial indebtedness to Tai. One of my ex-May colleagues, who was equally close to Tai, and whom I had intimated of this development, quipped: 'Oh, Dele, looks like Tai has paid you your own share of inheritance!' I didn't find that funny at all!

I had to dip in my pockets to pay Tai back after ten years of the Dreamer's total default. Tai never allowed this incidence to strain my relationship with him. When I reminded him of the event, he merely shrugged and told me to pay back when most comfortable for me. He further told me of the confidence he reposed in me. He reassured me that very soon I would not need to borrow from anybody because I would have made it in a big way. His policy, he reminded me, was never to lend money to anyone whom he knew had no ability to be ever financially independent.

And there was the occasion of my wedding to my soulmate and sweetheart, Jummy, in October, 1990. I had no car for the preliminary runs to be formally introduced to my numerous in-laws to be in the various western Nigeria locations. When Tai learned of my predicament, he made his driver as well as his best personal car available to me. To cap this, he honoured me with his presence by being present at the church service to witness the ceremony and he attended the reception as a special guest of honour as the Father of the Day at the high table. This was in Ile-Oluji, Ondo State.

DELE BABALOLA

LETTERS FROM TAI

Dr. Tai Solarin
1, Major Chukwuma Kaduna Nzeogwu Road,
Ikenne, Ogun State, Nigeria

Jan 6, 1982

Dear Dele,

Thank you for your letter of Dec. 8, 1981 which, after all, inched its way in last week!

Congratulations for your birthday lecture. It reads, to me, like putting you into the orbit to link hands with humanity's great.

All the very best.

PART OF A LETTER TO THE AUTHOR
HANDWRITTEN BY TAI, 1982

2

Dr. Tai Solarin

1, Major Chukwuma Kaduna Nzeogwu Road,
Ikenne, Ogun State, Nigeria

October 14th, 1982

My dear Bola,

Just got your letter of September
27th.

I cannot remember ever lending
you some money. If you are sure I did, well,
you could hold on to 50% of it and whenever you
can, pay the other 50%.

You seem to be getting quite a bit
running along your not-so-easy medical course.
This is the time, my young man, when you should
ride on all waves and yet keep afloat.

All the very best.

Very sincerely,

Tai Solarin.
P.S. Nearly forgot to say we are all well,
Sheila and all.

Dr. Tai Solarin

1, Major Chukwuma Kaduna Nzeogwu Road,
Ikenne, Ogun State, Nigeria

February 23rd., 1982.

My dear Dele,

Just a word or two to thank you
for your letter of February 2nd., and to say
we have no option but to turn the full heat
on/now on. Spades should no more go by any
euphemistic names.

All the best, my young man.

And don't work too 'ard.

Yours sincerely,

Tai Solarin.

DR. TAI SOLARIN
1, Major Chukwuma Kaduna Nzeogwu Road,
P. O. Box 150 Ikenne Ogun State.
Nigeria.

3

18th January, 1992

Dr. Dele Babalola,
Box 140,
Medical Centre,
Ajaokuta Steel Company,
Kogi State.

Dear Dele,

Just a few words to acknowledge your letter of
xii. l. 1992. I'm dealing with a deluge of letters
on the People's Bank affair.

Hope you do eventually win your way to U. S. Hanna
has eventually made it – last December 30, 1991.

All the very best, my young man, whatever you find
yourself doing.

Yours sincerely,

Tai Solarin

The Beginning Of The End

BY TAI SOLARIN

So the army is not going to go back to its barracks on January 14, 1976, after all. I decided to hold on to its reins of the government of Nigeria because "a large number of well and responsible Nigerians from all walks of life and from all parts of this country, as well as well-w of Nigeria at home and abroad have called attention to the lack of wisdom and the dangers inl in adhering to the target date previously announced." '62

We, honest citizens of this country, would like to know who these anonymous, responsible ci of this country are whose advice to the military government became so much more important the audible expressions of the common people of Nigeria.

There is only one anvil on which the acceptability of a government could be tested. That, : society, is the incorruptibility of that government. The Head of State has, himself, way back in said in downright honesty, that we had never had it so bad in our country. It is only much so today. And Tarka completely knocked the bottom out of the whole show by challenging the cc to dare probe him. Should he be probed, he would expose all the other men who deserved s probe, too, he vaunted.

Till now the whole world looks on askance - will Tarka be probed? On this issue alone lie credibility or otherwise of a new lease of life to the army regime.

There is nothing whatsoever today to justify the elongation, by a single day, of the army regim this federation.

"This nation is greater than any of us or any of its component units. There is not a single o us who does not need this country more than the country needs him. It follows, therefore, tha nation's survival as a united, virile entity and its real development and progress should, of necessit the concern of all of us over and above both our personal narrow interest and the interest of part groups or sections."

Very true, and that is why the army should not, in spite of the mortuary of wreckage in its think that it is indispensable in salvaging this country from its present throes. With eight years of rimental government with almost three of its nine-point programme accomplished, the army is prett spent and it would be inhuman to expect it to pull out a new trick to save this nation within two or the next two hundred years. ,63

What the army has succeeded in doing is in inheriting the ominous and leprous legacy of Ni governments never giving up voluntarily.

But we must record here that the aggressive wish to continue to rule at any price is not univ shared by the army hierarchy. Only like yesterday, Governor Ogbemudia said he would only be too p to go back to the barracks in 1976. Governor Esuene said it would be ungallant for the army to out of its word of honour to hand over the government to the civilians in 1976.

The army came to power because the people wanted it in power. It is in the interest of the itself that it should quit power when the people thought they have had its fill. An actor steps c stage whilst the ovation from the audience is loudest. To wait for that ovation to peter out to nothii before stepping off is, to put it the crude way, allowing the latrine fly to meet the bush toiletin; yet toileting.

Tafawa Balewa's government waited until it was forced out. Ironsi's government waited until shown the way out. We do not want the unsavory history to repeat itself in the life of the present goverr

Unless the military government has the courage to call it quits on January 14, 1976, a chain of might be set in motion, the end of which nobody would be able to predict. It would not be the c our beginning; it would be the beginning of our end.

Mayflower School,
IKENNE,
October 4, 1974.

DR. TAI SOLARIN

5

THE TIME TO SPEAK IS NOW

Nigeria is burning right now. Anybody who does not accept this verdict is either blind or deaf, or a fool, or all combined.

The Black American magazine, EBONY published, in its May issue, some trenchant and unpalatable revelations about our president. Nigerian Government has banned that issue of the magazine, but in spite, of the ban, it has burst in through crevices that were made available through private subscribers into the magazine. The contents of that issue, poignant and blood curdling, on the untold wealth of our leaders moored in foreign lands, have been revealed.

If the charges are wild allegations against the presiden and his lieutenants, the president should go on the air TODAY and tell the nation so. He should do more. He should sue the publishers of EBONY, releasing to this nation every document that has to do with the law suit. It is imperative that both should happen TODAY.

In the meantime, I swear, on behalf of all Nigerians who agree with me that we will not tolerate any group of army lads who, in a desperate wish to rule this nation, should want to stage a coup. We, the people of Nigeria, will rise up as one man and chase such men away.

If General Babangida challenges EBONY today, he should continue to lead us till 1992. If he capitulates, he should go on the air and tell us he allows an interim government to take over.

Long live Nigeria!

Tai Solarin.

80

DELE BABALOLA

DR. TAI SOLARIN
1, Major Chukwuma Kaduna Nzeogwu Road,
P. O. Box 150 Ikenne Ogun State.
Nigeria.

8th October, 1990.

The American Embassy,
L a gos.

DR. DELE BABALOLA

I have known Dele Babalola for seventeen years.
He was (1973 - 78) one of my students when he
proved himself an "egg-head". He is very
versatile, and easily the best read and most
prolific writer in his class.

He read medicine at Obafemi Awolowo University
at Ile-Ife. I have no doubt that Nigeria has
in Dele Babalola, one of tomorrow's very eminent
of doctors. He has got what it takes to make
abundantly good. He is paying his first visit
to the U. **S.** He will benefit immeasurably by
the exercise.

Tai Solarin
Founder and 1st Principal,
Mayflower School;
Chairman,
People's Bank of Nigeria.

People's Bank Of Nigeria

Ref: HO/PBK/CH/373

Date: November 6, 1990

Head Office:
28, Bajulaiye Road,
Shomolu, Lagos.
Telephone: 524357

His Highness,
The Ooni of Ife,
Ile-Ife.

Kabiyesi,

DR. DELE BABALOLA

Dr. Dele Babalola, an Ex-May, as we affectionately refer to every product of Mayflower School, belongs to a set that rings an un-ending bell in me. In its third year, I grew acquainted with several of the students in the class, especially a quartet that included Dele Babalola, distinguishing itself in its services, especially in its post-secondary days, by returning to school to teach maths and the sciences gratuitously to new generations of students that lacked teachers, not only in its Alma Mater, but also in Community High School in town where Sheila Solarin, erstwhile teacher of English to the quartet was now the headmistress. Generally schools honour their students by the mere fact of giving them admission. Some students, however, do their schools honour by the fact of such admission. Dele is one such student. It is difficult to imagine to what a giddy height, and how illustriously a young man of Dele's exquisite qualities would serve. There is evidence that he has got all that it takes to make abundantly good.

Dele has been invited by Alma College to spend the period of mid-January to mid-February, 1991 as a guest, and to participate in the celebration of Black History. He will be talking about Mayflower School.

I also wish to seize this opportunity to congratulate Kabiyesi on the 10th Anniversary. K'ade pe lori ki bata pe lese!

Tai Solarin,
B.A. (Manchester),
Dip. Ed. (London),
D.,Litt (Hon.) Alma College, Michigan.
Chairman, People's Bank of Nigeria.

DELE BABALOLA

YOUR REF:

OUR REF: G/M. 2005/7/TV/1.

MAYFLOWER SCHOOL
IKENNE
VIA SHAGAMU
NIGERIA

July 21st, 1979.

<u>To Whom It May Concern</u>

DAIDELA BABALOLA came into this school in September 1972 as a Class One student. He completed his course in July 1979 topping it with the West African School Certificate Examination which he should pass in Grade I at least.

He was academically sound and this won him the Oyo State post-primary scholarship.

Dele's faith in the dignity of labour needs no qualifications. He tried his hands at the dirtiest jobs on the school compound. He was for many years in the sanitary section of the school. He scrubbed, bathrooms, latrines and gutters. In his fourth year, he was a Medical officer. As a Medical Officer he had to clean sores remove vomittings of sick students and administer pills to them. He also laboured on the school farm and on the citrus fields.

He possessed immense organising abilities with the knack for good leadership. The students recognised this in him and so voted overwhelmingly for him as the second Senior Prefect in his final year at school. He was as just and firm Senior Prefect.

His mastery of the English Language is superb. He is a budding novelist. His amateur works in form of plays and novels are stunning and interesting. This natural qualities automatically made him the Chief Editor of the Mayflower Times.

Dele is one of the beautiful "feathers" in the "cap" of Mayflower and we do not doubt his success in life. We wish him well.

TFO/JOO.

T.F.O. Odubanjo,
PRINCIPAL, Odubanjo,
MAYFLOWER SCHOOL IKENNE 1.

83

THE AUTHOR RECEIVING THE HUMANITARIAN AWARD
FROM EX-MAYS GLOBAL CHARITY EX-PRESIDENT
DR. LANRE GBADEHAN, NIGERIA 2015

PERSONAL BENEFITS OF THE MAYFLOWER EXPERIENCE

I am sharing some personal experiences in this chapter on how the Mayflower training I received has helped me through life.

I must start by expressing immense gratitude to Tai for emblazoning it into my being that *I CAN BECOME WHATEVER I CHOOSE TO BE* and for giving us a song to celebrate that great truism:

We can become whatever we choose to be
No kings, no lords, no knaves can say us nay
For we believe that man is a potential doctor

Or lawyer or crook or dwarf or giant
Whichever he sets his mind to be.

We shall be giants
And therefore
We shall work
And work
And work
And work
Even if we must work
Work our fingers to the bone,
So may it be!

Any human being who can inspire a child and make that child believe that he or she has unique extraordinary abilities with which to attain any goals the mind sets itself, that person is a very great human being. And this was Tai *par excellence.* I can therefore understand why Tai was so bitter about the fellow Nigerian he met in Manchester in the forties when he (Tai) was struggling to gain admission into Manchester University in England.

The story was that when Tai was battling with mathematics, as reported in his autobiography, *To Mother with Love,* he requested the assistance of this fellow Yoruba countryman who by then had already gained admission to Manchester and was a senior student of some sort. Tai was weak in mathematics and needed help. Countryman tried to coach Tai but, apparently, he was too impatient with Tai and was not prepared to give him a chance to learn before delivering the near-crushing sledgehammer of his own hastily-formed and prejudiced verdict on Tai's mental ability. He declared that Tai's cerebral endowment was inferior and that people of his calibre were not fit to gain admission into the university! Tai ducked that 'wrecking blow'. He refused to believe he was doomed to fate. He bought mathematics books, pored over the worked examples and devoured the exercises. He would recall that he did not for once have to bend his knees in prayer to God to pass that matriculation examination. 'If only man can believe in his inner power,' Tai had muttered through clenched teeth, waving his fists in the air!

For Tai, passing the matriculation exam was an eye-opener to his innate abilities. He would therefore recommend the same method to any human being. The summary was that nothing short of bulldog tenacity, when applied to any situation at hand, irrespective of one's intellectual attribute or physical handicap, would take one onto the crest of the wave of success. Helen Keller was deaf, dumb, and blind and yet achieved greatness as an educator. Stephen Hawking (author of *A Brief History of Time*), perhaps the greatest theoretical physicist of our age since Albert Einstein, despite being physically challenged with motor neurone disease, (amyotrophic lateral sclerosis type) that confines him crippled to the wheelchair, was able to become the intellectual giant he is today. Think again of Ludwig van Beethoven, one of the greatest classical music composers, who was deaf and could not hear the great music he was producing! If only Man could believe in himself.

I differ from Tai in that I believe in God. God made man in His image so He gave Man creative imagination which man usually fails to use. With creative imagination and focused diligence, nothing is impossible. Chief Obafemi Awolowo also proved this in his heyday. He would stand every morning facing the mirror creating a mental picture of himself as a great Nigerian political leader. He would address himself this way – calling into existence by faith what at the time was only still ingrained in the imagination. He had believed it was going to be realized in his life time and had persevered and laboured assiduously to achieve this laudable goal despite all the impediments he faced on the way. He lived to be the first Premier of the Western Region of Nigeria in the 1950s and the Vice Chairman of the Federal Executive Council and Federal Commissioner for Finance during the General Gowon military administration of the late sixties and early seventies.

Tai had inspired me to bestir myself and make ample use of my time. While I was in Mayflower, I loved and applied myself to the written word that c a m e m y w a y and devoured writers like Wole Soyinka, Thomas Paine, William Shakespeare, Chinua Achebe, Mark Twain, Ernest Hemingway, Thomas Hardy, D.O. Fagunwa, Adebayo Faleti and several others at that tender age. Mayflower was such a fertile ground for me and my creative seedling therefore wasted no time in shooting up quickly. I was also beginning to try my hands at drama, poetry and novels by the time I graduated from Mayflower School. Tai taught me that leadership meant suffering and I had found myself in several leadership positions simply because Tai had been such a great inspiration. This is only using my situation as an example to explain how the training in Mayflower had toughened us for the years ahead. There are several of my colleagues who had similar experiences.

When the economic and political climate was unbearable at the time of Mr. Abacha, I decided to seek my fortune overseas. I planned to go to a Caribbean island, and Jamaica came readily to mind. I did not receive any offer of employment in the mail. I did not even know anyone in that country, apart from Bob Marley, whom I knew only through his music and nothing else besides; and even then, as at 1995, the year in question, Bob was long dead! The odds against my traveling were really formidable. But I kept focused and refused to give up.

I decided to apply Tai's method of dogged tenacity. I did not even have my airfare, and I was married and had three daughters then. But I had a goal as well as a vision and believed in my ability. I was able to travel to Jamaica by the tortuous route of journeying by road first to Cotonou and by Aeroflot flight from there to Malta in the Mediterranean. I left Malta for Moscow. After two severely cold winter nights in Moscow, I flew west, first to the Republic of Ireland, and then to Havana in Castro's Cuba! I spent three weeks of severe trial and privation in Havana before I secured the visa to enter Jamaica. In Jamaica, I endured unemployment for three months before eventually securing a job in a medical facility. This persistence and doggedness paid off for me on the long run. Thanks to my Mayflower discipline!

I had to use my creative imagination to survive, founding and running my own medical clinic in Barbardos, despite initial stiff opposition, and later grabbing a great New Zealand opportunity where I was able to buy into a prime New Zealand urban medical practice, becoming one of the principal medical directors. I never ceased looking for opportunities, and another one came in 2011 with a big upfront capital payment, transferring my services to the Perth region of Western Australia as an independent consultant GP.

Indeed, there is nothing impossible for a determined man who sets his face like flint and works very hard to achieve his highly focused creative imagination.

I believe this was how Wole Soyinka won the Nobel Prize for Literature, how Albert Einstein discovered the Special

Theory of Relativity, how Warren Buffet became the greatest world investor, how Bills Gates invented Microsoft, how Steve Jobs gave us Apple, and what makes Oprah Winfrey such a great TV talk show personality. The list goes on...

A microscopic fraction of the sun's rays, if focused on a diamond via converging lens, can burn through this hardest substance known to man.

TAI SOLARIN: LESSONS FOR NIGERIA'S YESTERDAY, TODAY AND TOMORROW

It is going to be very difficult for Nigeria to produce another Tai Solarin in our lifetime. Nigeria certainly wasted tapping the talents and sagacity of Tai to the fullest. There are several lessons to be learnt in the rich life of Tai.

He was born to peasant parents who could barely make ends meet, in Ikenne. Father was a polygamist, lacked ambition and was a lover and great consumer of the local liquor. Mother was a visionary – dreamt and was determined to get Tai educated at all costs, even if she had to give him priority over his twin sister, Kehinde. Money was scarce and so Tai had to be trained under various guardianships in the extended family. He eventually gained admission to Wesley College, Ibadan.

While in Wesley College as earlier reported in this work, he had torpedoed a corrupt tradition where students given 'chop' money had cheated repeatedly in purchasing foodstuff for the students. When it was Tai's turn, he had exposed this corrupt practice and spent every penny judiciously so that every student was superbly fed and there was enough meat to go round for the first time in the history of the institution! This proved that corruption as a social ailment, has been with Nigeria for a long time.

After his teacher training stint, Tai taught in various missionary schools as a pupil teacher. He had to go to church as well in the burning sun! Up to this stage in his life Tai was a nominal Christian and was a little timid and still struggling with the acceptance of the concept of God. He was getting disturbed that he would kneel down and pray and that several times God would not answer his prayers. He was therefore beginning to question if God really existed.

By a stroke of luck, he got a job as a typist at the Customs in Lagos and by a bigger stroke managed to get enlisted among the few Nigerians chosen to fight WWII for the RAF (Royal Air Force). He had sailed on the *Tuareg* to Britain, and witnessed air combat as a pilot. He survived the war and took up the RAF on its promise to give him free university education if he served and lived after the battles. Tai was demobilized in Canada. He travelled to London, studied hard and gained admission to Manchester University to read History and Geography. He had dreamt of obtaining a university education. The first university in Nigeria, University of Ibadan, would open its gates for the first time to admit students in 1948. As expected, it was a very competitive institution to gain admission to. The RAF therefore had presented a very good opportunity of which Tai was glad that he had grasped.

Tai lived in poor areas of London, and the Moss Side, near Manchester University, living with English landladies, and thereby cultivating the British way of life. He would later meet Sheila, and it was love at first sight. In Sheila, Tai had seen brawn, beauty and great intellect, all superbly combined in one very unique individual. They had a very simple marriage in London, and they would soon set out for Nigeria to found Mayflower after his short stint at Molusi College.

It can only take a Tai to found Mayflower, and without the support and fortitude of a Sheila, Tai would probably have aborted the Mayflower dream.

Mayflower was the passion of Tai's life: an opportunity for him to impact the lives of young Nigerians: to have a practical education that would make them ever employable for life, to be good at using both brains and brawn.

At various times, Tai would extend his educational mission to the greater society – like taking the police to court regarding the *ogogoro* (illicit gin) issue. The ogogoro was the local brew, the equivalent of the Russian vodka or the British gin. Tai was a teetotaller. Despite this he felt it was wrong for the government to tolerate foreign gin importation on one hand and yet banning the local equivalent on the other. It was declared illegal to be caught with the local gin. Tai purchased two bottles of ogogoro and presented himself to the police station to be arrested. He fought his battle from there and won. The gin is now no longer banned.

Among his several social crusades, he exposed the evil general surgeon in Sagamu who was abusing and exploiting his patients for detestable personal gains; physically removed decaying corpses of fellow citizens from the roads where they had been run over by 'hit and run' drivers; challenging sharp commercial practices that exploited the people's ignorance. Regarding the commercial bit, I remember him challenging an international tea company regarding why its bags could hardly produce a cup of tea in Nigeria whereas overseas the same bag would produce up to four or more cups! Tai had rendered several more services. Those mentioned represented only a tip of the iceberg. And there were the several newspaper articles that

Tai would write to correct and critique and castigate erring corrupt government officials and governmental policies, sometimes at great risk to his personal safety.

Tai had been a most focused individual. He wanted to educate the Nigerian child to believe in himself or herself and not to be afraid of anything or anyone; that fear was a mere distraction from progress; that anyone could become whatever he or she desired to be; that it only took a great deal of industry and, literally, whacking one's brain and body up for the great tasks ahead. Tai's life itself was more than an ample example – from very humble beginnings he had ascended to national and m o d e s t international eminence as a great humanist, ombudsman, teacher and educationist.

In retrospect, Tai had been like the proverbial elephant that blind Nigerians could only appreciate in parts and not as a complete entity. Some remember him as a dogged atheist; others as a God-sent ombudsman of the downtrodden and underprivileged; to some he was unrepentantly anti-government and anti-establishment; to some he was the principal of Molusi and then of Mayflower School, Ikenne and yet to some he was the first Chairman of the People's Bank. And the list goes on...

If only Nigerians could appreciate the complete Tai's core values: what he represented and his undiluted dream for Nigeria: Nigeria would be a much better place to live in today than it had ever been. This is because appreciating Tai would mean coming into close grasp with the problems shackling the Nigerian society and taking steps to ameliorate these hindrances. To understand what Tai stood for, therefore, would unravel 'the trouble with Nigeria', as

Chinua Achebe had put it in one of his books with the same title. No wonder Tai had been aptly described as the 'conscience of the nation'.

In 2015, Nigerians would rally round the opposition APC (All Progressives Congress) party to vote out President Goodluck Jonathan of the ruling PDP (People's Democratic Party). Nigerians had been frustrated with the lacklustre performance and profligacy of the incumbent regime and had preferred the Spartan, transparent, accountable and prudent alternative change to government that General Muhammad Buhari had promised at the polls. This was a very important landmark in the history of Nigeria – the voters looking beyond ethnicity and religion to vote in a presidential candidate based on his personal integrity and moral values only.

PAST

This immediate past is dated, for the purpose of this discussion, from 1952, when Tai returned to Nigeria from Britain, to July 1994 when he died. The present started from when Tai died to date. The future starts from tomorrow and extends into days and years to come. In other words Tai's life has become a reference point. His death marked the end of an era. No wonder Tai had been referred to variously as 'the anti-corruption crusader'; 'regular customer of the police'; the *'ogogoro* champion'; 'the corpse collector'; 'senior advocate of the people'- indeed the list goes on *ad infinitum.* Tai was the saviour sent to help rescue Nigeria from her pathetic educational system in the schools but, unfortunately, he was soundly rejected. He was the prophet not accorded due respect and recognition at home!

Right from the time Tai completed his university education, armed with B.A. Hons in History and Geography from Manchester University and a diploma in education from the University of London, he was through with formal education and he had a very clear idea of what he wanted to do with his life in Nigeria. He did not pursue a Master's course like Sheila or go further to Ph.D.; yet Tai was a very deep, logical, constructive and more importantly, an original thinker. He was the principal of Molusi College for about three years before going ahead to found Mayflower with his wife.

The first lesson learnt from Tai during this period was that Nigeria was too religious. Religion was not a deterrent to the progress of nations, properly speaking. It is noteworthy that the founding founders of the great United States of America were godfearing Christians and great achievers. They were the celebrated Thomas Jefferson, Benjamin Franklin, the second President, John Adams and the first President, George Washington. Their religion did not debar their progress. Although the USA had been named 'God's Own Country', in reality it is 'Man's Own Country'. Those pioneers were sincere and committed to serving God and the American people. Tai's concern was that Nigeria was latching on *lazily* to religion as the panacea for all her troubles, neglecting hard work and perspiration.

Tai's diagnosis of the national malaise was that rather than solving national problems, government and the politicians in power, would rather prefer to pray about them. If there was corruption in the country, the answer to stop it would be prayers and more prayers. If there was a problem concerning the erratic supply of water and electricity, it was a return to prayer again. Name the problem; prayer would solve it. This jarred Tai hard in his sensibilities. He believed the average Nigerian needed to do more work and physical exertion to improve self and country than lazing, kneeling and hoping prayer would replace diligence and forthright industry Even the Christian Bible decried laziness. Proverbs 13:4 declared: 'The soul of the sluggard desireth, and hath nothing: but the soul of the diligent shall be made fat.' While other nations, apparently worked on relentlessly to improve the quality of life of their people, Tai observed that in Nigeria, too much disproportionate time had been taken up by prayers where industry, vision, acute sense of mission, selflessness, creativity, self-denial, fortitude and perseverance should have been amply substituted.

Tai also noticed that people generally preached religion but were not really practising what they were preaching. With all the preaching, for instance, there should be love among the various ethnic groups that make up the country. But this was not the case. The Christian religion appeared to be a mere lip service in which people did not practice what they preach to others. He was aghast that some pastors and church members would lie, cheat, bribe, engage in several wicked acts, misappropriate church funds, commit adultery and fornication with church members Tai frowned at the idea of leaving the schools in the hands of the missions for he believed whoever had the nation's youths had the future and that it was important to catch the nation's children young with practical secular indoctrination like his rather than religious education that so far had proved unproductive for the country.

The other lesson was that Tai wanted technical education incorporated into our educational system. This advice was belatedly heeded by the Nigerian government. Tai had been advocating this since the fifties. He advocated that any student turned out of the Nigerian secondary education mill should be able to prove useful in a variety of vocations. He also pressed for compulsory military training of sorts - that students might end up being very disciplined, having been exposed to the harsh realities of life. Tai knew how important his own training as a combatant with the Royal Air Force was to his understanding of the art of survival. In Mayflower, he introduced the annual 'Education for Self-Reliance programme' during which students were sent to live for a weekend in the local jungle with only two unripe plantains supplied by the school for the 48-hour ordeal. Boys would go first, followed by the girls shortly after the latter's triumphant return. It was an experience that had helped many Mayflower students hatch survival strategies making something from nothing; making plenty from very little.

Societal projects have been mentioned earlier in this book. These represent technical education in action in Mayflower. The students were plumbers, electricians, welders, typists, and others. They took on these extra activities despite a full and rich academic curriculum. It made their education richer. It was not unusual for a Mayflower graduate become a medical doctor or pharmacist or some other professional, and still double as a technician to fix technically related problems in the course of their domestic or professional engagements. Tai's argument was that if technical education was part of the education of the student, it would be very difficult for that student to be unemployed in life. A metallurgical engineer, for instance, who found no ready formal employment, could easily set up shop as a self-employed plumber or an electrician while waiting for a job opening in his engineering field.

The other lesson learnt from Tai was that our leaders were not suffering with the masses. They lived a lifestyle that alienated them from the people that they were expected to serve. They rode the most expensive limousines and barricaded themselves in citadels that cost a fortune to build and maintain from the national treasury. If the leaders did not suffer with the people, they would not appreciate the peoples' pain, apprehension, needs and so forth. This would explain why the electricity and water supply in Nigeria is still erratic to date. The official projection, regarding these basic utilities, into the 21st century is grossly off-target. The Nigerian population, which is in excess of one hundred and fifty million people, grossly exceeds the capacity of the water and electricity supply. This situation is definitely unacceptable.

In *CIA World Factbook* (January, 2014), of 217 countries studied worldwide, regarding kWh of electricity per capita of population, Iceland topped the list with 51,142.11, USA was rated 10th with 12,185.94, Australia 16th (9,485.68), New Zealand 17th (9,259.6) and Nigeria a dismal distant 186th position with 115.04 kWh per capita! This is akin to practically living in the Stone Age! Tai had once asked in righteous indignation, *'When will Nigeria brace up to catch up with the rest of progressive humanity?'*

Education, Tai had insisted, was the inalienable right of every Nigerian child. This education should be available free and compulsory up to secondary level and free to all and sundry up to the tertiary level as well. In saying this, Tai never advocated that the general quality of education should be affected by this mass education programme. He was convinced that one could educate the whole world to the just below the exalted level of a University of Cambridge undergraduate in a lifetime, if only there was the will on the part of the educators. He believed in cost-cutting programmes that would in no way hamper the quality of education. For instance, the buildings did not have to be grandiose and too expensive and he condemned the Unity Schools and military Command Schools that he felt were spending too much to educate a select and over-pampered elite. He believed this should not be the case in a republic.

Tai would turn in his grave to learn of the outrageous salaries and allowances Nigerian legislators were earning in the 4th Republic under President Goodluck Jonathan. According to *Nairaland Forum* (January 21, 2011), in a Nigeria bereft of sound social infrastructures, where access to good education was financially very expensive for the common man, where public health care facilities were in shambles, where the minimum annual wage was pegged at a paltry N234,000 (about $1,300 US dollars in 2011), a Nigerian senator, on the contrary, earned 182 million naira (about 1 million US dollars) per annum. Effectively, the national minimum wage is 0.13 % of the legislator's annual take home pay! The situation, unfortunately, is not different today. It is no wonder that Nigeria, although rich and blessed with a lot of natural resources, is still a very poor country by the world's wealth standards. The present skewed wealth distribution is unrealistic and unsustainable. It should be torpedoed.

Tai also lived his life as a personal example for others. He lived what he preached and he urged Nigerian leaders to do no less. If Tai offered you sand as food this was because he was prepared to eat it with you and not the other way round. The late political sage, Chief Obafemi Awolowo, had aptly described Tai as one of the greatest exemplars of our time. Mayflower School was an educational experiment that succeeded and which other Nigerian schools would do well to copy rightly. Mayflower had proved more relevant today to the reality of Nigerian life than 'Ivy League' schools like King's College, Queens' School, and International School, for instance. The statistics and quality of products of the schools, when juxtaposed with similar assessments of Mayflower graduates, should prove my point.

It would appear that the named prestigious schools probably produced more people in government, law and the judiciary than Mayflower School. On the other hand, Mayflower seemed to take the lead in producing potential entrepreneurs, scientists, doctors, farmers, nurses, technicians. A large research into this area is overdue to accept or debunk the above assertion. Tai once challenged the whole of Africa to debunk his statement that Mayflower had produced the first female chemical engineer on the continent. No one has challenged this claim to date as far as I know.

The table on the next page, however, amply demonstrates the present superb quality of the academic performance in Mayflower School in the recent secondary school leaving certificate examination.

Mayflower Private School's WASSCE May/June 2013 Result Summary
(from the Mayflower Private Secondary School Website)

No.	Subjects	Total No. of Candidates	No. of A1-C6	% of A1-C6	No. of D7 & E8	No. of F9
1.	English Language	218	216	99.1	02	00
2.	Mathematics	218	201	92.2	17	00
3.	Yoruba	213	182	85.4	26	05
4.	Economics	211	207	98.1	04	00
5.	Geography	164	128	78	33	03
6.	Physics	118	109	92.4	09	00
7.	Chemistry	118	114	96.6	04	00
8.	Biology	218	215	98.6	03	00
9.	Agric. Science	085	085	100	00	00
10.	Financial Account	052	052	100	00	00
11.	Commerce	052	050	96.2	02	00
12.	Government	100	093	93	07	00
13.	History	048	045	93.8	03	00
14.	Literature	054	035	64.8	18	01
15.	Home management	042	040	95.2	01	01
16.	Technical drawing	029	025	86.2	02	02
17.	Further Maths	008	008	100	00	00

The standard keeps improving. There was nothing close to this during the period Tai was in charge although the signs and promises were there. It only proves that the school was laid on a very firm foundation and it has not floundered but still blossoming. Indeed, the best is yet to come!

One other lesson from Tai was the correctness of that saying that in a very corrupt country where honest men were few and far in between, then the rightful place for the honest man would be prison. Several times, Tai had faced the indignity of prison confinements with equanimity. He had proved that the pen was mightier than the sword. His article, *The Beginning of the End,* which was one of the major forces that truncated the Gowon regime and which landed him for a period in the Nigerian gulag in 1974 is hereby reproduced for posterity:

So the army is not going back to its barracks on January 14, 1976, after all. It has decided to hold on to its reins of the government of Nigeria because 'a large number of well-meaning and responsible Nigerians from all walks of life and from all parts of this country, as well as well-wishers of Nigeria at home and abroad have called attention to the lack of wisdom and the dangers inherent in adhering to the target date previously announced.'

We honest citizens of this country, would like to know who these anonymous, responsible citizens of this country are, whose advice to the military government became so much more important than the audible expressions of the common people of Nigeria.

There is only one anvil on which the acceptability of a government could be tested. That, in any society, is the incorruptibility of that government. The Head of State has, himself, way back in 1970, said in downright honesty, that we had never had it so bad in our country. It is only much more so today. And Tarka completely knocked out the bottom out of the whole show by challenging the country to dare probe him. Should he be probed, he would expose all the other men who deserved such a probe, too, he vaunted.

Till now, the whole world looks on askance - will Tarka be probed? On this issue alone lies the credibility or otherwise of a new lease of life to the army regime.

There is nothing whatsoever today to justify the elongation, by a single day, of the army regime over this federation.

This nation is greater than any of us or any of its component units. There is not a single one of us who does not need this country more than the country needs him. It follows, therefore, that the nation's survival as a united, virile entity and its real development and progress should, of necessity, be the concern of all of us over and above both our personal narrow interest and the interest of particular groups or sections.

Very true, and that is why the army should not, in spite of the mortuary of wreckage in its trail, think that it is indispensable in salvaging this country from its present throes. With eight years of experimental government with almost three of its nine-point programme accomplished, the army is pretty well spent and it would be inhuman to expect it to pull out a new trick to save this nation within two years or the next two hundred years.

What the army has succeeded in doing is inheriting the ominous and leprous legacy of Nigerian governments never giving up voluntarily.

But we must record here that the aggressive wish to continue to rule at any price is not universally shared by the military hierarchy. Only like yesterday, Governor Ogbemudia said he would only be too pleased to go back to the barracks in 1976.

Governor Esuene said it would be ungallant for the army to back out of its word of honor to hand over the government to the civilians in 1976.

The army came to power because the people wanted it in power. It is in the interest of the army itself that it should quit power when the people thought that they have had its fill. An actor steps off the stage whilst the ovation from the audience is loudest. To wait for that ovation to peter out to nothingness before stepping off is, to put it the crude way, allowing the latrine fly to meet the bush toileting man yet toileting.

Tafawa Balewa's government waited until it was forced out. Ironsi's government waited until it was shown the way out. We do not want the unsavory history to repeat itself in the life of the present government.

Unless the military government has the courage to call it quits on January 14, 1976, a chain of events might be set in motion, the end of which nobody would be able to predict. It would not be the end of our beginning; it would be the beginning of our end.

PRESENT

The greatest lesson of the present is that we have not, as a nation, hearkened to Tai's teachings. There is still a lot of greed and selfishness in our political leaders. Basic infrastructures still don't work in Nigeria. Our roads are still in deplorable states. Electricity and water are still luxuries that only the very rich could afford on a regular basis. Fixed telephone and fax services are still lagging behind - although the influx of cellular mobile phones has modified this problem but at an intolerably expensive price relative to the average person's earning power.

The quality of public education is at its nadir. Quality education is now a major investment in the life of the child that only very few parents and guardians can afford. This is very sad. There is still a lot of religious intolerance in the country, claiming lives in several hundreds. There must be a way to eliminate the Boko Haram scourge permanently.

Loving one's neighbour as self is far from Tai's ideal in Nigeria today. Ethnic identification is still largely preferred to the national identity. This is unacceptable and should be reversed.

The basic wage earned in the country today could not properly feed any human being. Despite this, a lot of the political leaders still loot millions of naira at the people's expense as already enunciated. The difference between their public earnings and those at the lowest rung of the ladder is, simply put, unjust. This is also unacceptable.

Our intellectual resources in human terms in the universities have deserted the shores of this country in hordes for greener pastures: 'the brain drain syndrome'. This anomaly should be addressed because the inputs of the intelligentsia are invaluable to our growth and progress as a nation.

The present youth of the country needed to be reassured that there is hope for them. This hope might be denied if Nigeria does not change its present course of political affairs and purposeless meandering.

In summary, therefore, Tai's ideals for an egalitarian society are far from being realized in Nigeria today and the consequences for the future are quite grim indeed.

THE FUTURE

The lesson for the future is very simple. Nigerians must build an egalitarian national structure and arise anew and refreshed like the phoenix, from the ashes of the present foibles if a meaningful future for the country is to be attained.

Only citizens who truly deserve honour should be honoured. Robber-politicians and "legislooters" in the political system must be weeded out completely and politics made financially unrewarding. It should be solely a vehicle of service to the people and not a shortcut for self-enrichment. Whoever mounts the soapbox and campaigning should be prepared to suffer for the people and strive to uplift their living standards. Is politics not supposed to be the art of the possible?

Talking of honour, in Tai's lifetime, no educational institution in Nigeria awarded him an honorary doctorate degree despite his herculean efforts in the field of education. He was not really appreciated and given his due recognition. Yet, in faraway U.S.A., the late Ronald Kapp, a professor of biology for thirty years and Vice-President for Academic Affairs (1969-1989) of Alma College, Michigan State, on behalf of his institution and humanity, recognized Tai's efforts. In 1971, Tai was invited to the college as a special guest and commencement speaker. He was also awarded an honorary doctorate of letters. Indeed, a prophet is never worthy of honour in his own home!

Only leaders who are ready to suffer with the people and uplift the people from their common suffering can give a hope and a true future.

Tai had prophesied that leadership is suffering. One cannot will it any other way – consider Jawaharlal Nehru and Mahatma Ghandi of India; Chief Obafemi Awolowo, General Murtala Muhammed and Alhaji Aminu Kano of Nigeria; Nelson Mandela of South Africa; Abraham Lincoln and John Fitzgerald Kennedy of the USA.

Does Nigeria have leaders who are prepared to suffer with the people today? Are the beautiful ones who will rule tomorrow born yet?

THE AUTHOR IN CAP, FAR BACK, AT THE EX-MAYS
GLOBAL CHARITY FUNCTION TO CELEBRATE SHEILA
SOLARIN (FRONT), LONDON, 2007

EX-MAYS, EX-MAYS' GLOBAL
CHARITY AND THE FUTURE OF
MAYFLOWER SCHOOL

As at the initial time of this writing (Sept. 17, 2010), old
students of Mayflower School, popularly called "ex-Mays",
have met for a first reunion of its kind in Tampa, Florida, at
the Grand Hyatt Hotel. Credit must be given to the energetic
and visionary men who birthed this idea and pursued its
realization with great zeal and zest. I place their names
here for posterity - Remi Ogunlari, Dr. Bashiru Dawodu,
Dr. Rasheed Oshokoya, Mr. Akin Ashekun, Dr. Daniel
Osaro, Dr. Emmanuel Lanre Uwagboe Gbadehan and Dr.

Abayomi Ojetunde. They are ex-Mays and, with the exception of Dr. Ojetunde, are based in the USA. Dr. Ojetunde is based in the UK. They have all done Mayflower proud.

Since this inaugural session, the charity has been formally registered as a non-profit organization in Iowa, USA (EIN 20-3853789). It has organized successful annual conventions in the USA (Tampa, Atlanta, Houston, Chicago, New Jersey and St. Anthonio; London, England (thrice) and Lagos, Nigeria (once).

Its tenth anniversary will be marked in Nigeria, Ijebu-Ode, in October 2015.

Dr. Osaro is a very energetic medical practitioner in self-employment. He has proved himself a great asset to the Iowa community, USA, where he is based as a healthcare provider. He has also proved greatly supportive to the cause of realizing the 'Mayflower Dream'. He is doubly certified in Family Practice and Emergency Medicine.

Dr. Uwagboe was on the attending staff of Harlem Hospital (College of Physicians and Surgeons, Columbia University, New York). He is a devoted academic medical professional in the field of gastroenterology and hepatology. Presently, he practises privately in Atlanta, Georgia, USA. He is passionate about getting Nigeria on her feet and feels that ex-Mays might be able to play a great role in this regard.

Dr. Ojetunde is a high-trajectory dreamer and achiever. He owns a network of dental clinics in the UK and has diversified into international real estate and aviation. He is the Director of Aviation Operations of Elysian Airlines based in

Yaounde, Cameroon. The airline services several West African countries such as Gambia, Cameroon, Guinea Conakry, Liberia, Ivory Coast, and Sierra Leone.

Dr. Bashiru Dawodu has also made good with his practice as a paediatrician in Mitchell County Pediatrics Centre, Camilla, Georgia, USA. and expanded into the real estate investment world.

Dr. Oshokoya, MD., MPH, is the CEO of Calvary Health Support Inc., Miami, Florida, USA. He is also an adjunct professor at Miami Dade College, Florida.

Remi Ogunlari is a chartered accountant and Head of I/A at Arcelor Mittal in Chicago. He had also attended Roosevelt University in Chicago.

Mr. Akin Ashekun was the first *pro tem* Chairman of Ex-Mays' Global Charity. He is a venture capitalist and private equity specialist. Currently, he is managing partner with Pyur Holdings Inc., in the Tampa/ St. Petersburg areas of Florida, USA. He was the former Senior Vice President for Gunallen Financial and Chief Financial Officer for the Kenedee Group.

All these men are ex-Mays. They are still young. They are pace-setters and amply demonstrate the high-flying quality of the products of Mayflower School.

Ex-Mays Globarity Charity has been registered in Iowa, USA, as a charitable organization, thanks to the fortitude and determination and financial support of the first elected Chairman and President, Dr. Daniel Osaro. The short-term goal of the charity is to raise in the nearest future a modest 100,000 US dollars or more to support Mayflower School – scholarship awards, infrastructural maintenance and rehabilitation; and the supply of laptops and computer educational software to the school amongst others. The long-term goals are still unfolding.

The idea of Education for Self-Reliance that Tai lived and died for is obviously growing from strength to strength as this is abundantly demonstrated during Ex-Mays' global conventions. This is another Tai's dream for the Nigerian youth coming true. It is refreshing to know that the Mayflower idea is not only alive, that it is thriving, kicking, running and going for gold! More grease to the collective elbows of ex-Mays all over the world as they blaze new trails in their various endeavours of expertise.

It seems to me that in the future, with Mayflower Secondary School firmly in the hands of the younger Solarins that ex-Mays might eventually run mutually-agreed joint projects to perpetually ensure that Mayflower never lacked any funds. This would ensure that only the best teachers are enrolled, that the library is well stocked with current titles and computerized; that ex-Mays would keep returning to the school to encourage discipline and to rekindle and maintain the beloved old Mayflower traditions.

PARADOXES

It occurred to me to highlight here the paradoxes I have observed in Tai's life.

The first is that the frail-looking Tai was a very mighty soldier whenever he welded his pen and ferociously attacked the various governments of the day: from Balewa to Akintola, to Gowon, to Shagari, to Buhari /Idiagbon, to Babangida. He must have sent shivers down the spines of nearly all of these men that had occupied the Nigerian version of the White House. Indeed, size or stature, with regards to Tai's physical frame, had nothing to do with it!

Tai argued for the two-child family and he had two children himself and encouraged the propagating of small family units and communes in Nigeria. The thrust of the argument was that a manageable population was easier to feed, shelter, treat and educate. Of course, this was too tough for the average Nigerian family to practice. In reality, Tai had turned out to be the Nigerian with the greatest number of children - albeit adopted! Tai must have taken over the responsibility of looking over about five hundred or more of other people's children!

Tai was never a professional journalist but he must have written more newspaper articles than any Nigerian journalist alive!

One could also state that he was probably the most honest Nigerian of his time. Despite this achievement, he was sent to prison like a common criminal for constructively criticizing Nigerian governments several times too many. In one prison in Northern Nigeria, he ate the tough hide of camel meat, which broke a few of his teeth!

It was ironic that the Nigerian educational system continued to reel from one level of maladministration and bad planning to the other with a seasoned educationist like Tai totally ignored.

He was ready to take on the responsibility of a total overhaul of the system without demanding a salary!

The apparent unspiritual and ungodly Tai had turned out to be the most loving, morally-sound and transparently honest Nigerian of his time. Members of the Nigerian clergy often stood in awe of Tai's impeccable standard of morals, punctuality and ethics.

A cursory look at Tai would identify him easily with suffering humanity He dressed like one; looked like one but that was where it ended. He was the Nigerian who invested 100% of his intellect and a great deal of personal funds in the education of Nigerian youths who hold the future of Nigeria in their collective hands. In so doing, Tai became financially poor that these youths might be rich and at his transition, Tai had become the wealthiest Nigerian because the seeds he had sown in the youths have now started to bear fruits! The harvests projected are very rich indeed!

Without becoming a didactic academic of the ivory-tower mould, Tai was able to nurture his intellect to show very strong influences from Thomas Paine, Bertrand Russell,

Jean-Jacques Rousseau, Aristotle, Herbert George Wells and Winston Churchill, all rolled into one being, of his time. His intellectual well was very deep and full of rich educational resources indeed. And he was still our *Oga Tasere!*

ONE AREA OF DISAGREEMENT

I wish to place on record that I disagree with Tai in the area of his denying the existence of God.

He himself started out as a devoted Methodist Christian and dumped God when he felt that God did not seem to be hearing and answering his prayers. As pupil teacher in the forties, he had prayed that he did not want to be posted to rural Iperu but to the more acceptable urban Lagos. He had ended up in Iperu! How could God have done this to him?

In Canada, after being demobilized by the Royal Air Force, he had planned to pursue his university education there. He had thought it would be easy to share the roof of fellow white Canadian Christians. But the Christians had let him down because they didn't feel it would be a great idea to shelter a black-skinned man! This racial rejection had hurt Tai to the marrow. It would hurt anyone in his shoes. Again, Tai was mad with God here!

In England, as discussed elsewhere in this book, a fellow Nigerian in Manchester who was a Christian had told him his brain was inferior and that he should return to Nigeria to take up some humble task!

It is my submission that Tai had focused on individuals and people to castigate God, concluding that there could be no God because bad people had failed him! But then bad people could never translate to a bad God. I believe God is good all the time.

And the universe is full of the evidence of deity - that this world could not have been created by an accident as the Big Bang Theory had alluded. The human foetus has the lung, alimentary canal, limbs etc. formed long before delivery with the use of these organs. Think about this organization and orderliness for a minute.

The world around us is guided by strict laws which we cannot break without great consequences. Water freezes at zero degree of Centigrade under the right conditions of pressure and volume. An aeroplane obeys the laws of aerodynamics. If this law fails, a plane crashes! The law of gravity is real. If one disputes it and jumps off a cliff's edge, he has himself to blame! If the world ticks through an intelligent design, there has to be a great Designer. This Designer is God!

The planets, stars, moons, asteroids all course through space with a regularity that obeys physical and mathematical formulae. They are not rotating and revolving by accident or trial and error motions! They do not crash into each other at random!

I started questioning the reality of God after I left Mayflower School. Before then I had shared Tai's belief in agnosticism and/or atheism. I continued to be uncomfortable in my agnostic coat as I grew older and as I read more and started forming my own independent opinions.

I had to shed this coat finally when I realized just like matter is made of gaseous, liquid, and solid states that man also has three parts which are mutually inclusive - the body, the soul and the spirit. The soul is the seat of intelligence or the mind. The spirit is not easily discerned. What happens when we sleep and dream? What happens when we have hunches or premonitions? I submit that these are spiritual experiences. I have witnessed people with demonic possessions and who have been delivered of same. I have seen people oppressed under witchcraft. Again, these are spiritual phenomena. The fact that one cannot see the wind does not mean that wind does not exist. One can feel it!

I remember one night when I was in Mayflower. We were preparing for the School Cert. Exam. In the same room with me were Omole, Ogayemi and Kamson. There was no electricity when I woke up early in the morning. I sensed that there was something dangerous in the room. The room itself was pitch dark and I could not even make out the outline of my nose!

I cautiously got off the bed, avoiding the part of the floor, where one knew by instinct that my slippers were. It was customary for me to wear them as soon as I rose from sleep. That very day something guided me not to do that. I could feel goose pimples all over as my hairs stood on end!

I carefully groped for the hurricane lantern on a nearby table, lit it and searched for my slippers. Crawled into one of the pair was a big dark scorpion with the tail raised ready to strike and sting! I quickly struck it dead with a cudgel nearby. In no time I alerted my colleagues about the event. Ogayemi was amazed and said, 'Man, seems you have some serious spiritual fortification!'

What could have warned me about the presence of that danger? Extra-sensory perception? Spiritual awareness?

My being a Christian today happened as a personal spiritual experience but the full gist of it is beyond the scope of this book. I believe there is God and that man owes it a duty to himself to relate to Him or not to. It is a matter of choice. I therefore have no problems with Madame Solarin or Tai himself denying the existence of God. Our experiences are different. We are all mortal and still learning and that is why I recommend that the reader who wants to read further on this subject should seek out the book titled *Creation* by the world-acclaimed researcher Grant Jeffrey. This book can be ordered according to the information presented in the Further Reading section. I have read it and find it very informative. I strongly recommend it to the reader.

I know of two highly rated Nigerian mathematicians who are world-renowned evangelists and pastors. Mathematicians, as we know, have sharp wits and minds. They are not easily fooled. They are deep and logical thinkers. Now, if two topmost mathematicians conclude that there is a God, if one is an unbeliever, it makes sense to reconsider one's opinion on the strength of this alone. I am referring to no other men of God than Pastor Enoch Adejare Adeboye of the Redeemed Christian Church of God and of Pastor William Folorunso Kumuyi of the Deeper Life Ministry. Pastor Kumuyi had passed through Tai's Mayflower – as a student and later, as a teacher!

CELEBRANTS ON FREEDOM WALK FOR TAI SOLARIN, IN
FRONT OF HIS STATUE, YABA, LAGOS, 2014.

EX-MAYS MUST CONTINUE TO
ASSIST EACH OTHER

Many times people have asked me why I give so much of my
time to serving Mayflower causes. I always smile because they
do not understand what I know.

The fact is Mayflower is like a big family and we as ex-
Mays always look up to Tai and Sheila for inspiration and
examples. We love their lifestyle. We loved the way they had
nurtured us in Mayflower. We knew that they had
given us practical education for surviving anywhere in this
world. They had bestirred us to know that the only factor
that could stop us from achieving a successful life was
ourselves. They taught us that we had all that it took to
make it in life. They taught us to take pain and promised
pleasure would

come. They taught us how to hang on to our visions and dreams without chickening out too soon and they guaranteed us victory if we had patience and were steadfast and creatively diligent.

I have personally gained so much for being an ex-May and I wish to seize this forum to thank some ex-Mays who have proved very supportive to me at critical moments in my life.

I start with the group of friends I first made at Mayflower and still keep now. I salute Femi Adewumi, Wale Omole, Kayode Kamson, Mathew Ogayemi. We are more than biological brothers – always there for each other. I remember them because they encouraged me to look inwards and brought out the best in my person. They encouraged me to be a leader, a writer and to be fearless. I will always be there for them as well.

Omole visited me in Barbados after holidaying in Las Vegas, Nevada, USA, in 2001.

I spent time with Kamson with my family in his home in Plumstead near London, UK, in the summer of 2003. He treated us like royalty.

Femi hosted me in his new house in Ibadan in 2004. He honoured me as if I was the President of the United States.

I remember Kunle Odunsi, who always played the role of big brother and has always been an inspiration. He encouraged me to take appointment as senior prefect in my set. In university, he saved me money to buy my prelim books by freely giving me those he had used the previous year. He has always been on the look-out for my welfare and I appreciate him. I am particularly glad for him because he has worked so hard and has reached a great level of professional achievement in medicine. He is today a medical giant. He has the unique distinction of having the FRCOG of the UK, a PhD from medical research at Oxford University, a graduate of Yale University where he did his O&G residency and now a director of research, an attending and full Professor at Roswell Park Cancer Research Institute in Buffalo, New York. Kunle's research interest is in the area of developing biological markers for detecting early ovarian cancer. Not too long ago, he made the news when he received a grant of $700,000 towards one of his numerous researches. I believe he is on the way to becoming a Nobel Prize winner in Medicine, in the nearest future. I salute him.

I thank Kemi Osude, my classmate, and now an attorney in the UK. She is also an international business executive, presently based at home in Ilisan, Nigeria, as a director of a big social events organizing company. I met her in 1995, at a critical moment, when I needed foreign exchange to fund my trip out of Nigeria in search of greener pastures.

Without hesitation, she loaned me a thousand US dollars which looked like a billion dollars then. She believed so much in my ability and had encouraged me to press on to greater heights. I appreciate her.

Kazeem Bokini is another classmate, a business magnate based in Nigeria. At my difficult hour, he pressed a gift of 20,000 naira in my hands as his widow's mite, to support seeking my fortune in greener pastures. I thank him.

I am glad today that I did not disappoint these well-meaning supporters. I have paid back all the loans and I am grateful to them all.

We must continue to be kind to each other, sensitive to each other's needs and be selfless in our support to reaching out and helping out.

In a nutshell, I am glad I went to Mayflower School. I am glad I was taught by the Solarins. I consider it a privilege to have met the ex-Mays in my life. I desire wholeheartedly that this book will be a blessing in one way or the other to the reader.

Tai dreamt of being counted among the four greatest Nigerians that ever lived by the time of his death. I believe he achieved this goal in his lifetime. I believe he was highly qualified because he served Nigerians with everything he had, more than anyone ever did.

FURTHER READING

Tai Solarin: His Life, Ideas and Accomplishments; Richard Carrier; internet source: http://www.infidels.org/library/modern/richard_carrier/Tai_Solarin.html

Merry Mayflower, Melodious Community, Swinging United - collection of school songs marking 40th- 45th anniversary.

To Mother With Love; autobiography; Tai Solarin, 1987; Board Publications, Ibadan.

Tai and Sheila; biography; Dele Babalola, 1981; Oyerinde Printing Press, Ibadan.

Tai Solarin s Footprints; Wale Omole, 1994; Inland Printing & Publishers, Lagos.

Mayflower, The Story of a School; Tai Solarin, 1970; John West Publications, Lagos.

Education for Greatness VolI; collection of great educational speeches by Tai Solarin; Sulaiman Bola- Babs. Great Books Publishing, VI, Lagos, Nigeria, 2001.

The Open Sore of a Continent: A Personal Narrative of the Nigerian Crisis; Wole Soyinka; New York: Oxford University Press, 1996.

Towards Nigeria s Moral Self Government; Tai Solarin, 1959.

A Message for Young Nigerians; Tai Solarin, 1980; Macmillan Publishers, Lagos.

Timeless Tai: A Collection of Tai Solarin's Articles on Education; ed. Akinbayo Adenubi, 1985; F & A Publishers, Lagos.

Mother is Gold; Adrian Roscoe; Cambridge University Press, 1971.

The Man Died; Wole Soyinka; Rex Collins; 1972.

Who's Afraid of Solarin? Femi Osofisan, 1978; drama; Scholars' Press, Calabar.

Creation; Grant Jeffrey; 2003. ISBN 0-921714-78-5. A great book. A must-read book for any inquiring mind who wants to know the truth about the origin of man and the entire universe. For ordering information and pricing contact: Frontier Research Publications; P.O. Box 129. Station 'U\ Toronto, Ontario M8Z5M4. In the US call 1-800-883-1812 and Canada call 1-800-853-1423.

Morning Yet On Creation Day; Chinua Achebe; London Heinemann, 1975.

The Trouble with Nigeria; Chinua Achebe; London, Heinemann, 1984.

Black Man's Dilemma; Revised Edition; Chief Areoye Oyebola; Board Publications Ltd., Ibadan, Nigeria.

ABOUT THE AUTHOR

THE AUTHOR SPEAKING AT AN EX-MAYS GLOBAL
CHARITY CONFERENCE IN IJEBU-ODE, NIGERIA, 2015

Dr. Dele Babalola was born on Dec. 16, 1961, in Maiduguri, Northern Nigeria. He was educated at Mayflower School, Ikenne, (Sept. 1973 - June 1978); University of Ife (now Obafemi Awolowo University, Ile-Ife; from Sept. 1978 – June 1986). After a stint of medical internship at the University of Ife Teaching Hospitals Complex, National Youth Service at the Medical Centre, Ajaokuta Steel Company and a short period of private practice at Midway Hospital, Ile-Ife, he became the physician-in-charge of Okene Clinic/Hospital in Lagos, Nigeria (1992-1995).

From late 1995 he transferred his medical services overseas. He first worked in Kingston Public Hospital/Victoria Jubilee Hospital, Jamaica (March 1996-Feb 1997). Next in tow was his appointment as a Registrar GP at the Psychiatric Hospital, Barbados (April 1997 –April 1999).

After this, he was engaged as a Clinical Medical Officer of Health at Black Rock Polyclinic, Barbados (April 1999-April 2002). By July 2000 he established his own private GP practice and named it First Foundation Clinic Inc.

Dr. Babalola is a natural writer, a talent he cultivated and nourished while in Mayflower where he had written plays for the stage, prose and numerous articles for the school *Mayflower Times* and *Winslow* magazines.

He was appointed into several leadership roles while in Mayflower – senior prefect, medical officer, President Young Farmers' Club, Editor-in-Chief of *Mayflower Times*. In the university, he edited *Winslow the 30th* and *The Ex-May*, the journal of old students of Mayflower in higher institutions of learning nation-wide. In 1984, he was the President of NASEM (National Association of Student Ex-Mays), President of Mayflower Old Students' Association (Unife Chapter) and President, Ife University Medical Students' Association. In 2000, he was elected General Secretary of Caribbean-African Association of Barbados and in 2005 he was elected into the Executive Council of Barbados Association of Medical Practitioners.

He has a number of publications to his credit – *The Drinkard's Song* (a poem in pidgin English published in *Okike*, 1976, and Donatus Nwoga's anthology of poems, *Rhythm of Creation*), *Tai and Sheila* (1981), *The Pull of Blood* (1998, 2006), *Oga Tasere (2004)*, *My Walk with God* (2006) and *Your Personal Health Guide* (2006).

Dele has been actively involved with Ex-Mays Global Charity/Global Ex-Mays Alumni Association since 2005. He is presently the Editor-in-Chief of *Ex-Mays Global Magazine* (four editions produced to date) and Global Vice-President for Oceania and Asia. Presently residing in Perth, Western Australia, he is a consultant GP and a Fellow of the Royal New Zealand College of Medical Practitioners and Royal Australia College of General Practitioners. He is married to Jumoke, a registered nurse of Murdoch University, Australia. The marriage is blessed with five lovely children, 3 girls (Oyin, Ola, and Ebun) and two boys (David and Joshua).

PRAISE FOR TAI SOLARIN

"Many thanks for your thoughtfulness in presenting me with a copy of *Oga Tasere*. Writing the book at all, in honour of Tai's memory is another act of thoughtfulness, for which I greatly commend you. It certainly brings back memories of that doughty fighter and educational exemplar. Congratulations..."

WOLE SOYINKA, CELEBRATED NOBEL PRIZE WINNER, ON 'OGA TASERE' EDITION OF *TAI SOLARIN*.

"It was the middle of the night, and there I was, bellowing out old Mayflower songs, singing along, full throated with the words thoughtfully reproduced in Dele Babalola's moving and evocative tribute to Tai Solarin, the visionary founder of Mayflower School, a revolutionary educational institution at Ikenne. Memories came flooding back, and although tinged with some guilt, I was transported many, many, many, years back to those fun-packed, mischief-filled, rebellious, but powerfully influential formative years at Mayflower School. My house guests, whom I had woken up, came knocking on my door wondering if I was alright..."

PROFESSOR OMOFOLABO AJAYI, KANSAS UNVERSITY, USA

" In Babalola's rendering, Solarin and his school become a symbolic manifestation of Nigeria itself, one that can illuminate both the nation's past and its potential for the future..."

KIRKUS REVIEW

"Babalola can tell a good story....*Tai Solarin* introduces readers to a man who sacrificed much for the betterment of his country....the spirit of the story is powerful..."

BLUEINK REVIEW

"Those unfamiliar with Solarin will get a quick introduction to this important figure in Nigerian history, but those who were personally touched by him will find this book to be a warm, nostalgic journey of remembrance."

CLARION REVIEW

"Dele Babalola...has written the most admiring and comprehensive and personal biography of Tai Solarin and his school...as a historian, I value works like this. "

RICHARD CARRIER, FREETHOUGHTBLOG.COM

Made in the USA
Columbia, SC
21 September 2022

67271117R10086